Two Infinities

Leslie Belitz

Two Infinities

A MEMOIR OF LOVE AND CHILDHOOD CANCER

Leslie Belitz

To order additional copies of this book, contact:
Xlibris
1-888-795-4274
www.Xlibris.com
Orders@Xlibris.com
786030

Contents

PART TWO

I dedicate this book to Kaitlyn.
You enchanted me for five years.
Your spirit lives.

Acknowledgments

A few weeks after Kaitlyn died, I announced I would write a book about her short and meaningful life. I am grateful to friends and family who accepted my endeavor with love and encouragement.

I would like to thank several talented people who assisted me on a journey to write a book that shares my heart and honors Kaitlyn.

Jean Gibson, who carried my original manuscript home to have the first viewing and offer her expertise as a reader. Robert Spiegel, who offered suggestions and encouragement to keep writing my story. The people from the Apple Store who guided me on computer skills. Rica Caro, the publishing consultant who made a connection with me from our first contact. Jerry Belitz, who read the entire manuscript and offered wise suggestions to enhance the story. And Elizabeth Belitz, my daughter and best friend. You birthed the amazing Kaitlyn. I am proud to be your mother and share this journey with you. Our team continues in love and light.

Kaitlyn Gem

Grandma, I see a dead bird on our path. I want to pick it
up and kiss it goodbye. I need to tell the bird something
special. "You are beautiful, bird. I love you. Goodbye."
Okay, Grandma. Let's go to the park.

The bird was a small, black-and-yellow finch that appeared to have recently
died. It was quite plump and looked asleep on the ground.

Kaitlyn squatted close to the bird to speak directly into its ear.

She was a light like no other little human. She was my granddaughter,
my best friend, my teacher. Her wisdom was clear. Talk about a teaching
moment. We were a great team. I set the ground rules, the setting was
there, and Kaitlyn taught me how to love, accept, and move forward.

The significance of this lesson was about to be revealed.

The Beginning

My granddaughter's name was Kaitlyn. She entered the world on May 22, 2012, at nine minutes after midnight, weighing eight pounds, nine ounces. Her mother, my daughter, Elizabeth, was in labor about sixteen hours, while I was waiting outside the door. I was looking into the window of the hospital labor and delivery room when Kaitlyn arrived.

When Kaitlyn was born, I watched her lock eyes with her mommy, and the two souls bonded in a familiar and forever love. She passed all the tests to be a beautiful, strong, and healthy little girl. Kaitlyn had blue eyes like mine and dark hair like her mom. Her eyes were wide open, proving her to be an alert child, ready to take on the challenges of life.

We were thrilled to have this new person enter our family. She broke out of the blanket she was swaddled in, spreading her arms wide open to the world. We had no clue that this precious person would only live five and a half years and that she would develop a cancerous tumor in her brain stem, a diagnosis referred to as DIPG (diffuse intrinsic pontine glioma). It is a rare cancer that affects approximately three hundred children each year.

But its rareness was meaningless because it happened to my grandchild 100 percent. The world I knew, the one that highlighted Kaitlyn as the shining star, ended on November 21, 2017. That was the day she succumbed to the horrible symptoms of this disease, and Kaitlyn took her last breath.

The Day Our World Changed

When Kaitlyn woke up on April 19, 2017, she appeared confused and struggled with her abilities to walk, speak, or control her bladder. Elizabeth called me, and I heard panic in her voice as she described Kaitlyn's symptoms. My daughter's distress caused me to react quickly and get to their house as fast as possible. I observed what Elizabeth had already seen.

Kaitlyn struggled with her ability to speak and move the right side of her body. Something was very wrong. She had not been feeling well for the past few days, suffering from what appeared to be a stomach virus and a headache. The week before these annoying yet seemingly benign symptoms, Kaitlyn had happily attended a piano lesson, soccer practice, preschool, and swimming classes. But this morning, she exhibited extreme symptoms unlike those of an ordinary childhood illness. We feared that Kaitlyn had suffered a trauma to her head. We called for an ambulance and an assessment by medical professionals. The emergency medical team arrived promptly and recommended that Kaitlyn and Elizabeth go to the hospital immediately via ambulance. I would meet them there with my husband.

Kaitlyn Gem

Grandma, I want you to climb into the bed with me. They will push the bed and give us both a ride. I will make room for you to be with me. I am happy you are here.

Kaitlyn was given medications to help her relax and cooperate. She smiled a crooked grin that revealed a partially paralyzed face. When she spoke, her words were mumbled, but I clearly understood her message. The medications influenced her mood; however, my familiar embrace gave her comfort. I know I felt safer feeling her body close and wrapping my arms around her in a loving and familiar hug.

The Hospital Shock

The medical interview and exam in the emergency room prompted the doctor to request a head-scan evaluation.

Kaitlyn was uncooperative and unhappy about having to undergo a brain scan. My grandma instincts revealed that she was quite frightened as she started her day with loss of body functions and an ambulance ride to a hospital and then was told by strangers to remain still as they put her into a machine for a procedure that she had never encountered. Her behaviors were consistent with a four-year-old child's fears in a strange and unfamiliar environment. She refused to cooperate when asked to stay still and enter a chamber for the brain scan. The medical team had to sedate her to obtain the images required for her evaluation. We soon discovered that Kaitlyn had a high tolerance for these drugs and needed multiple medications to achieve the desired goal.

Kaitlyn remained true to herself in the hospital setting. She was an expressive child filled with facts and opinions. She protested being asked to do things she did not understand and absolutely refused to comply. Her personality and pride remained intact, even with the diagnosis about to be revealed.

She screamed, "No, leave me alone. You are hurting me." Her words were loud and garbled because of her impaired speech, but her intention was clear. This was no place for a happy and healthy child. The world as she knew it was entering a new dimension, and she was going to protest it all the way.

The emergency room doctor came to us with the results. She looked at my daughter and cried as she reported that the scan pictures revealed a mass in the brain stem. The doctor told us they would transport Kaitlyn and Elizabeth by ambulance to another hospital that was better equipped in the treatment of childhood brain cancer. My daughter looked like she had been shot in the heart; in that instant, I could see her heart was broken.

I walked up to my child and hugged her. I was in shock and totally confused. My mind told me, *It can't be brain cancer. It must be a mistake. It must be a urinary tract infection or asthma.*

Those illnesses were unpleasant, but we could get her medicine, and she would recover.

Elizabeth asked me to call Kaitlyn's dad. They had been divorced for several years, and she did not want to tell him the news. She asked me to call him, and I did. I told him where to meet us. I told him Kaitlyn was very sick. I cried as I explained they thought she had brain cancer.

Kaitlyn Gem

Grandma, guess what? The hospital has a room for children with a million toys. We can check it out tomorrow when I feel better. They have toys for all ages. You can watch me play or play with me just like at your house. We will have fun at the interesting playroom.

Kaitlyn always enjoyed keeping busy with toys that excited her imagination and captured her interest. Her bright spirit shone even in an intensive care hospital bed. I listened to Kaitlyn tell me about the new experience she was planning for us tomorrow. She found life to be an interesting and happy adventure. She was an active participant in her life journey.

The Dreaded Cancer
Umbrella

On April 19, 2017, the life Kaitlyn knew and enjoyed dissolved, and her end-of-life journey began.

Kaitlyn and her mom were taken to the hospital that would be Kaitlyn's home for the next seventeen days. She was given a second evaluation in the next hospital emergency room setting and then admitted to the pediatric intensive care unit. We spent the day with Kaitlyn, attempting to comprehend her health situation while entertaining and comforting her in this new and strange place.

My mind raced with questions, thoughts, and a strong sense of denial while attempting to comprehend the situation. It was too big to grasp. Could this really be happening to Kaitlyn? Was there a cure for this type of cancer? Of course, we would get her the best care and treatment possible. There were advances in cancer care every day.

My thoughts were hopeful when I interacted with Kaitlyn and read her books or played with toys she enjoyed. She was impaired in her speaking and walking. The right side of her body was stiff and weak. But she was still Kaitlyn. Her essence shone through even with her body impairments. I couldn't escape that we were in a hospital room in the intensive care unit. My emotions were random tidal waves that flooded me with sadness, anger, and disbelief. I looked at Kaitlyn, saw my beautiful granddaughter with her big blue eyes, and imagined her closing them forever. I couldn't conceive of the world without her. She was my superstar. She brightened my days with her love, thoughts, unique perceptions, activities, and busy schedule.

Elizabeth loved her child, and they needed each other to have an enriched world. They were eternal friends meant to share life's journey together. How dare cancer interfere with the unique bond shared by a mother and daughter?

Kaitlyn's family needed her vibrant spirit. She enhanced all of us with her marvelous perceptions and humorous views of the world. One day she declared, "When I grow up, I'm going to name my baby Banana." We were constantly entertained by her happy proclamations.

What about Kaitlyn? She had friends, plans, and dreams. She had much to learn, goals to achieve, and many firsts in life to experience. She was just beginning.

Thinking about the implications of the cancer diagnosis was unbearable; they were impossible to fully comprehended. That day at the hospital, I functioned as a stunned person. We were forced into a world that contained no clarity under the dreaded umbrella called *cancer*.

I anxiously waited to speak with the doctor assigned to her case. I was desperately seeking answers to all my questions regarding Kaitlyn's health. *When will she be well enough to go home and live just as we did yesterday? How did this happen? Can it be a mistake? What can be done to make cancer go away?* Finally, sometime after dinner, we gathered to meet with the oncologist in a private conference area to discuss the situation. I was grateful to be included in this discussion because I was the grandmother and these conversations were usually reserved for parents. I sat at a table and attempted to comprehend the oncologist's words. He explained the DIPG diagnosis and treatment options and said the next action would be a brain biopsy in the morning. He told us about other hospitals that offered care for childhood brain cancer. Kaitlyn's parents agreed to remain at home and proceed with treatment here.

Kaitlyn loved her family and friends, and everyone would be here to support her. She was facing a tremendous adjustment to her life, and staying in her familiar setting would be less burdensome on her emotional health. I heard words spoken in the room, but I struggled to fully accept the meaning and magnitude of Kaitlyn's diagnosis. I held onto last week's memory when Kaitlyn was seemingly healthy and living as a happy four-year-old child. But I heard the truth. Kaitlyn had a cancer that was deadly. I was now the grandmother of a dying child and the mother to a young woman facing the death of her little girl.

I met with my husband when the meeting concluded to share what I could recall. I spoke in fragments, piecing together what I heard, "Kaitlyn has DIPG, and it cannot be cured. It is a deadly brain cancer. Kaitlyn will get treatment here, so she can be at home surrounded by family and friends. A brain biopsy is scheduled for the morning. A brain biopsy can be dangerous but is needed. There may be a chemotherapy treatment, and they may shrink the tumor with radiation." I rambled on and on, attempting to process and communicate the information. The one thing I knew for certain was that Kaitlyn was scheduled for a brain biopsy in the early morning. We needed to go home and get back as fast as possible.

We drove home in silence with our thoughts. We had been at the hospital for only one day, and it seemed like an eternity. Kaitlyn's existence was derailed when the sun rose that morning, impacting all the people who knew and loved her, but mostly impacting the young and beautiful life that she rightfully assumed was hers to live until completion. Children are usually sheltered from death and are rarely confronted with facing their own demise. I cried for my daughter facing the loss of her child. I thought about how unnatural this was. Children were not supposed to die. They were supposed to grow up and enjoy their childhood. Learning, fun, and new experiences should highlight their days. Their biggest problem should be choosing an ice cream flavor. We were facing this unthinkable event clouded in our belief that this horror does not happen to young people.

Kaitlyn had a malignant brain tumor that was ready to destroy her beautiful body and end her existence. The little human I loved was going to die soon, and there was nothing I could do to stop it. I felt completely powerless and heartbroken. I knew I needed to stay healthy for my girls. I needed to be fully present in the moment, so I could gather the courage and strength to live in this new world. I felt exhausted as I processed this truth. I hoped sleep would free me from this nightmare.

Elizabeth spent the night snuggling her child in the small hospital bed. My daughter had just been informed that the physical bond she and Kaitlyn shared was coming to an end. So the girls nestled and grasped each other, and Elizabeth knew these moments were precious gifts.

The surgical biopsy procedure took place in the early morning as promised. I was there to sit with my daughter as her baby experienced an operative brain probe. We now existed in the medical world that executed their own time schedule, vocabulary, and emotional compass. We were compelled to trust that their decisions, knowledge, and expertise would assist Kaitlyn in her sickness and restore her to the highest state of health possible for a child with this diagnosis.

I wondered how the biopsy was going to help her. I anticipated it would identify the cancer, so they could provide a way for Kaitlyn to live. The words spoken by the doctor eight hours earlier, informing us of the gravity of this tumor, escaped my mind as my grandma hopefulness rose to protect and save Kaitlyn. My brain fluctuated from hope to despair and back to hope. I clung to the prospect that if the cancer was identified, it could be matched with a chemotherapy treatment that could free Kaitlyn from this dreadful course. I was not a medical professional, but I was an intelligent grandmother who could use simple logic to solve this complex problem.

We waited to hear from the surgeon. When we saw the doctor, we were told Kaitlyn did well during the procedure and was in recovery. We were grateful we could be with her soon.

As I waited, I read about DIPG. I learned it is a tumor that grows in the brain stem and kills children. I read about it over and over, trying to comprehend the information and searching for any indication of hope for Kaitlyn's life. I read that before a child dies from this type of cancer, he or she will probably be robbed of the ability to speak, swallow, walk, and breathe. The end-of-life symptoms would rob Kaitlyn of the skills she worked so hard to obtain in her almost five years of living. Her beautiful voice would not be heard, laughing and singing would be over, her love of eating various foods would be constricted, and walking or running was going to cease.

I adored Kaitlyn from the second she was born and had cared for her since she was three months old while her parents worked. I thought about the upcoming year and how Kaitlyn's life would be affected. I remembered the plans for her to attend kindergarten and all the extracurricular activities I orchestrated to enrich her life. Prayers, questions, and deals with God flooded my brain and overwhelmed my entire being. I resorted to the cliché that I believe is the go-to for any person in my position: "Please, God, take me. Let Kaitlyn live."

I vowed to myself to provide Kaitlyn with the highest quality of life in facing her death. That was my commitment before the DIPG diagnosis. Kaitlyn was my world. I retired from working as a speech and language pathologist to watch Kaitlyn from her birth. I felt connected to her from the start of her life. Every day with her I attempted to provide an atmosphere of joy, love, and learning. I set up my home as a place designed for her comfort, safety, growth, and happiness.

As far as I was concerned, nothing changed as everything changed. I was going to continue loving Kaitlyn and give her a life filled with quality, love, and fun. I knew we would not have quantity. I was heartbroken that I would not see her grow up. I was totally ready to fill each moment of every day with unconditional love. I was her grandma, and Kaitlyn was my heart.

Kaitlyn Gem

Grandma, am I going to die? It is true that everyone dies. Old people usually die before children do. But very sick people die too. I hope I can live. I will try my best to stay alive.

Kaitlyn lost her innocence at four years old as a patient in the hospital and undergoing treatments reserved for terminally ill people. She was an insightful child and grasped the grave reality of the disease she was now forced to endure.

I validated her knowledge that she was sick and attempted to explain it in a child-friendly manner. I told her she had a bump in her head that caused many problems in her body. I told her the doctors, nurses, and her family were going to help her and try to shrink the unwelcome bump that was making her sick. I reassured Kaitlyn that her mommy and I would be with her to help her get well.

I told Kaitlyn that every day of life is precious, and we will always love each other, try to have fun, learn and grow, and continue to be the great team we already created. This bump was our new challenge.

Another Word for DIPG Is Death

Kaitlyn lived one day shy of reaching five and a half years old.

I learned from my amateur research on the internet that the survival rate for children diagnosed with DIPG is close to 0 percent. I read about one child who survived, and this gave me the hope I needed that if one person could live then two could survive. Reading about DIPG became my nighttime obsession. I was driven to find the solution to this impossible equation. The medical treatment consisted of radiation to the tumor in an effort to shrink the cancerous growth. I knew family and friends would assist the process with their prayers for quality of life, time, and a miracle cure.

My fears grew as I read about this murderous tumor. On every page, I deciphered that the monster grows and spreads and causes horrendous symptoms and eventually death. Every study deemed that in six to twenty-four months, Kaitlyn would die. I was heartsick and scared from my self-guided research on DIPG. My eyes couldn't escape the meaning of words that conveyed it was a fatal diagnosis. I glimpsed pictures of children with this affliction and wept as I saw their beautiful bodies transformed and barely recognizable. Their faces were large and round, and their frames seemed overgrown. Most of these children looked confined to wheelchairs or beds with expressions that conveyed their beautiful spirits trapped inside ailing bodies. Their eyes reflected the knowledge of their fates.

My mind still oscillated between acceptance and denial. I found it too difficult to conclude that Kaitlyn was chosen to join this group of innocent victims. Surgery was not an option because of the location of the tumor in the delicate area of the brain stem. I read about numerous chemotherapies for treatment of DIPG at various locations in the world. I indulged my heart with the possibility that a chemotherapy could be identified that would save my precious granddaughter, and she could live to tell this childhood tale. I fantasized about traveling with Kaitlyn and visiting healers and miracle workers. I was desperate, and Kaitlyn was in need of a divine intervention.

Elizabeth helped me face the reality of the situation using her wise mind, medical knowledge, and realistic, grounded presence. I learned that although there were considerable chemotherapies executed, they were classified as trials and were essentially in an experimental phase, offering no expectation of a cure. Everything else involved wishes and prayers that we could do here at home.

We had almost five years to believe Kaitlyn was a healthy child who would grow up and grace us with her beauty, brilliance, and love, and we had seven months to prepare Kaitlyn for her death. This book is a tribute to Kaitlyn from me, her grandmother. Kaitlyn called me Grandma. She was and will forever be my granddaughter.

Kaitlyn Gem

Grandma, the bump in my head is not like any sickness I ever had before. When my stomach hurt, I got better after I threw up a few times and ate gentle food for my tummy. When I had a bladder infection, the doctor gave me medicine, and I rested and quickly got well again. But this sickness is different. It's taking a long time to get better, and I'm not sure I will ever get better again.

Kaitlyn shared with me her keen perceptions of her illness and prognosis. I never lied to her about the outcome because I truthfully did not know the outcome. I read information and saw the odds, but I also read about miracles and hoped one would be granted to Kaitlyn.

Kaitlyn Gem

Grandma, did you bring the soup? Did you make a lot?
Did you bring the blueberries too? You love to cook
delicious food for me. I'm hungry. Can I have some now?

Kaitlyn and I loved to cook and eat together. Our daily routine usually
included two large meals and many snacks that we savored together. We
had thoughtful discussions as we ate bread, vegetable soup, and fruit salad.
Kaitlyn loved eating healthy food, as we had long conversations about our
plans for the day and the mysteries of the world.

The Hospital and a Child

Kaitlyn remained in the hospital for seventeen days. The first two nights she was admitted to the intensive care unit and then moved into a room on the pediatric special care unit. It was a confusing time. There seemed to be a continuous deluge of people who entered the room to probe and examine her and deliver information on Kaitlyn's health status. I did my best to listen and comprehend the information presented.

Kaitlyn regained her speaking and walking abilities. We didn't understand why but rejoiced in the return of her speech and motor skills. She boldly spoke to medical personnel, whom she viewed as intruders, "What is your name, and what do you want? If you touch me, I may bite you! I really want to go home."

She still needed to be stabilized medically, and a treatment plan had to be formulated before she could go home. Elizabeth and I needed a quick education on how to cope and care for a child with brain cancer.

Kaitlyn had moments of joy and episodes of tears. She had to endure necessary and sometimes painful procedures. She frequently protested prods as an intrusion on her body. She eventually complied, especially after a treat was promised or a little extra kindness was administered. Elizabeth slept in her bed with her each night. The mother-and-daughter team endured the nighttime interruptions common in a hospital setting. Meanwhile, they shared special moments that involved gentle whispers to each other, heightening and celebrating their bond.

Elizabeth returned home for a few hours during the day to shower and change clothes, while I stayed all day and left at night to get some rest and make chicken soup. I returned to the hospital in the morning with foods that connected Kaitlyn to the memory of wholeness. I reminded Kaitlyn of her life before being confined to a hospital room. A simple bowl of Grandma's chicken soup created a flash of enjoyment.

Kaitlyn's diagnosis and prognosis challenged everyone's humanity. The medical care was devoted to stabilizing her vital signs and helping her achieve a state of comfort while living with a brain tumor. They were powerless in their ability to cure Kaitlyn and assist in a positive outcome. We were all challenged to have courage while processing the impending death of a young child. I welcomed the display of compassion from the generous people who entered the hospital room. I appreciated the housekeeping woman who blew kisses to Kaitlyn and me and agreed to return after Kaitlyn's nap so she wouldn't disturb her rest. I admired the volunteers who gave their gift of time and brought joy to a child confined in a bed and delighted to have a new toy. We once got a visit from a lady and her little therapy dog. She put the animal on Kaitlyn's bed, and for a few precious moments, Kaitlyn was not a sick child but rather a little girl loving a dog.

So I made chicken soup for Kaitlyn to nourish her soul—to feed her love. It was a gift to my sweet granddaughter. I presumed my soup bypassed the tumor in her brain and went straight to her heart. My gift of devotion brought a smile to Kaitlyn's face, confirming her knowledge that Grandma's love was ever present. Perhaps the soup could heal her with love. The broth contained the remedy to nourish her being. As she ate, she was healed. She was happy. She was living. I was doing my Grandma job: to love Kaitlyn, to feed the essence that lived inside her, and to provide a space in time when cancer did not exist. We shared chicken soup, love, and nourishment. We blanked out the horrible diagnosis, physical pain, and dreadful prognosis. In our private time machine, we existed in a bubble of love. I smiled as Kaitlyn ate chicken soup created by me with the special ingredient called *love*.

Kaitlyn Gem

Grandma, I have something interesting to tell you. Mickey Mouse is not really a mouse. He's a person wearing a costume and pretending to be a quiet mouse. He never speaks. But he is fun to look at and hug. It's just like what we do on Halloween.

Grandma, today I was brave. There was no time to be shy. I got to let everyone in this room hear the song I love from my favorite singer Andy Mason. Now everyone can have a favorite song too. Today was the best day of my life.

Kaitlyn's hospital stay and illness caused us to cancel a Disneyland trip that Jerry and I had planned with Elizabeth to surprise Kaitlyn and celebrate her upcoming fifth birthday. Elizabeth's work friends arranged for Disney characters to visit us at the hospital as a gift to fill the void of our canceled trip. Their gift was given to offer us hope and joy in a bleak hospital room. The character Belle asked Kaitlyn to sing her favorite song. Kaitlyn looked at me and knew that she would sing the song she loved best: "Spring Chicken" by Andy Mason. She sang the entire song with a loud, proud, and brave voice. When the visit was over and hugs from Mickey Mouse and Minnie Mouse were done, Kaitlyn and I snuggled together and recalled the events of the day. We learned to be happy, give generously, and be brave even in a hospital room with a grim diagnosis.

My Name Is Kaitlyn

The hospital room became our home for more than two weeks. Kaitlyn spent most of the time in bed. Sometimes she looked out the window, and I told her stories of life outside the hospital. I often read books to her, and she developed an interest in chapter books. In spite of her brain tumor, Kaitlyn was learning. She took naps as I sat beside her, watching her beautiful face. I hoped she was having dreams of running and playing and being a healthy child. Did her dreams allow her to enter a world that restored her good health and gave her the freedom to live without cancer? Was there a dream world that freed her from her current waking existence?

Her dreams, conversations, and playtimes were frequently interrupted by hospital people needing to do their jobs. Kaitlyn had intravenous needles in her arms, a port in her chest, and limited use of her arms and legs. She needed help performing the simplest tasks that just a few weeks ago she could do with ease.

Her memory, awareness, and spirit were intact as she grieved for the skills she no longer mastered. Kaitlyn was determined to let every person who entered her room know that her name was Kaitlyn. She protested being called Katie, Princess, Kate, Pumpkin, Sunshine, or any other variation of her name. She seemed to have an intuitive sense that when someone was not calling her by her name, they were not really seeing her as an individual. They were doing a task and not regarding the beautiful person in front of them.

She loved the name Kaitlyn. She learned how to say it clearly and write it beautifully at a young age. She articulated her name with pride when introducing herself to a stranger. Kaitlyn understood that her name identified her. The name Kaitlyn was the second gift she received from her mother after Elizabeth gave her the gift of life.

Kaitlyn Gem

Grandma, I am ready to go home. The hospital is no place for a kid to have fun. The people who work at the hospital are very busy and always in a rush. The food is okay, but I like your food the best. You know what I love to eat and when to give it to me. The hospital people make you wait and wait. A person could starve! I want to go home and sleep in my bed, play with my toys, and enjoy my life. I will be more comfortable when I am home.

The long hospital stay was a tough experience to endure but provided a safety net and routine that we grew accustomed to. Elizabeth and I felt a healthy balance of fear and confidence as Kaitlyn was discharged from the confines of the hospital.

Kaitlyn looked at the room that had been her home for the past two weeks and proclaimed, "This place is done. I will take baths again at home. Grandma will move into our house. It is time to go where I belong. I never want to see you again. Goodbye, room."

We left the hospital setting with the responsibility to care for a child with brain cancer and all the known and unknown needs that coexisted with that circumstance and sorrow. We attempted to predict Kaitlyn's requirements for comfort and safety. We were ready to be out of the hospital and back to the environment that was home.

Between Hospital and Home

We filled my car with medicines, instructions, appointment dates for oncology doctor visits and radiation times, a wheelchair, a shower chair, a portable toilet, plants, stuffed animals, and other assorted goods and information that had accumulated in the hospital room.

As we left the bounds of the hospital room, a woman approached me and placed two children's books in my hand. I thanked her and slipped them into my bag containing the many things we had collected over the past two weeks. I glanced at the books at a stoplight and was taken aback when I scanned the small lettering printed on the bottom of the book: "How to discuss death with a child." I didn't view the second book. I quickly hid them in the glove compartment of my car. I was not about to read those books to Kaitlyn. I was not ready to accept this morbid outcome.

I had hope that Kaitlyn would survive. I expected the prayers uttered throughout the world would be heard by God, and a blessing would salvage Kaitlyn from her inescapable projected fate. I gripped tight to the notion that Kaitlyn would be the child to defy the medical statistics and not be a victim to DIPG. I was primed to be the grandmother who witnessed a spectacular miracle, and Kaitlyn would live.

Kaitlyn Gem

Grandma, it is great to be home. I was away a long time. I'm so happy to see my toys, bed, and clothes. You and Mommy will take care of me and help me get better.

The extra bedroom was set up for a guest and ready for me to move into. Kaitlyn accepted this transition as our new normal. She sensed her care was extensive and required extra help. Before her cancer diagnosis, I was at her house early in the morning when her mother went to work. Now I would sleep in the room next to her bedroom. I told her we could have a pajama party every night and visit each other's rooms whenever we wanted. We loved being together and were ready for this enhanced closeness.

The New Normal

I packed a small suitcase from my home and moved in with my girls. We were going to do this together with the support and love of the people ready to help.

We had a team of friends who became our angels on earth and helped us with meals, groceries, activities, and toys for the almost-five-year-old child. They gave us hugs, love, and encouragement. Visitors came and went throughout the days. Most were sensitive and respectful to Kaitlyn and the various mood swings of a five-year-old child coping with a brain tumor. My daughter took a leave from her job to spend all the time she could with Kaitlyn. She knew this meant an absence of money, but her commitment to Kaitlyn's care and their relationship took priority.

Elizabeth had to manage without having her regular salary to support herself and Kaitlyn. The constant bills of maintaining a house existed with the additional debts necessary to care for a terminally ill child. I respectfully revealed this on Facebook, and the response from people was astounding. There was a tremendous outpouring of generosity that flowed from the people who grasped the enormity of the situation and sincerely wanted to make an important impact. Elizabeth was freed to focus on her child and worry less about the payment of bills. People made brief home visits and put cash in Elizabeth's hand. Acquaintances sent cards with checks to help relieve the financial burdens imposed by the current circumstances. Anonymous donors sent cash and checks to support Elizabeth's quest to care for her child without the burden of financial worry. She graciously accepted the generosity of people. Each gift lessened the uncertainty about financial responsibilities and created space to fully care for Kaitlyn. She regarded each contribution with her grateful heart as offerings given to assist her during this devastating life course.

My daughter was forced into living the worst nightmare a person could possibly imagine. Every mother's dread became her reality. Our community supported her with the love attached to the offerings they bestowed.

Many nights before I went to sleep, I posted on Facebook an update of Kaitlyn's condition. It helped to believe I was connected to people in my broken and isolated world. The responses reinforced my purpose as a grandmother, mother, and caretaker. I felt loved and supported by anyone's willingness to respond with a like or a comment. It amazed me how even the smallest gesture carried what my heart needed. I looked for the simple words of love and encouragement and accepted them as big gifts sent from the soul.

My needs during this time were simple and complex: nutritious foods; a chance to shower, stretch, and meditate; and a hug and smile upon arriving and a kiss goodbye. Thankfully, most people who entered our world were gracious and intuitive and followed this unspoken plan like a well-tuned orchestra.

Sadly, a few people entered our world ill prepared to manage their intentions. I recall an encounter when a dad brought over his two young children, a delicious meal, and an expectation for a visit. He looked at Kaitlyn sitting on the couch and said, "Is that all she does?" Then he made a comment about her weight gain. I led him to the door and explained that Kaitlyn was a very sick little girl. I thanked him for the food and shut the door. I don't believe this man intended to do harm. His generosity was evident. I believe he was shocked when he saw Kaitlyn's appearance, and the words left his mouth too fast. To protect my peace, I had to protect myself from thoughtless comments. Maybe I also protected this man from making more comments he may have regretted in time.

Another person told me I should prewrite thank-you cards and leave them outside the house with a sign instructing visitors to take one. I made my own etiquette rules and tried to always be polite, but I suspended the time-consuming thank-you-card rule to communicate what I believed my friends already knew. I trusted that my heart was clearly expressed with my facial expressions and brief exchanges of words, as the Kaitlyn community glanced at the struggles and strengths required on this path.

Some of these negative encounters jolted and haunted me for a long time. The intensity of my situation and the needs of my girls were all I could handle. The needs of others had to be met by their other friends or family members. The people who did not understand this added a crack to my already broken heart. I served as the protector, witness, and guide for my daughter and granddaughter. I nourished their bodies, minds, and spirits on a daily basis. I had to leave behind the few people who were not willing to accept the intention of my walk.

I reminisce about the generous deeds of so many people who arrived to love us during this profoundly difficult time. The memories give warmth to my heart that beats with the cold void of sadness. Strangers appeared at the door with gifts of food, trinkets, smiles, and hugs. People wished us well with comments pertaining to our courageous hearts and unbreakable spirits. Kaitlyn proclaimed that each person who walked into our home was our new friend. I may not recall all the names or even the faces of each volunteer who furnished us with gracious offerings. I do know all contributions filled me with gratitude and strength to face another moment on this crossing.

I was eternally grateful to all the friends who showed up at our door.

Kaitlyn Gem

Grandma, I don't want anyone to talk to me or be near me.
It hurts my ears and makes me want to scream. It hurts
when people touch me. I do like when you or Mommy
massage my feet. It helps me rest and fall asleep.

Kaitlyn suffered greatly from pain—side effects of medicines, and
treatments. She was uninhibited about expressing her profound physical
and psychological pain. "Go away. I won't take my medicine," she shouted.
She wanted her misery and frustrations to be heard. "My head hurts. Leave
me alone." Her distress was evident with her piercing screams, loud cries,
and physical lashings at herself and us.

Elizabeth and I took care of our precious girl with love, humor, and
intuition. We supported each other through this uncharted territory. We
observed that her rare diagnosis caused a magnitude of physical and
psychological features requiring various medications and tremendous
flexibility.

We were grateful we had each other and the community of people who
embraced us. We told Kaitlyn we loved her several times a day. We threw
her noisy kisses when she didn't want to be touched. We hugged her when
she gave us permission and treasured each caress as a gift.

The Law and the Grandma

Grandpa Jerry, Elizabeth, and I were there by Kaitlyn's side for every radiation treatment, medical test, and oncology appointment. Jerry usually stayed in the waiting areas, while Elizabeth, Kaitlyn, and I went into the examining rooms for the various appointments.

When we went to the oncology clinic, we anticipated seeing one of the many oncologists on staff, a nurse, and perhaps other medical personnel visitors. On one occasion, the doctor took the time to talk to me about HIPAA laws. HIPAA is the acronym for Health Insurance Portability and Accountability Act, which limits who can receive health information about a patient. He explained that my request for clarification about Kaitlyn's treatment violated the medical setting rules. I was ashamed of my ignorance and realized I was displacing my anger onto the institution that was attempting to serve us during this ordeal. I openly wept as I couldn't control my tears from pouring out of my eyes. I cried for the emotional pain I felt from being forced to live in this horrendous situation. I cried for my granddaughter and the inescapable life trap she was in. I cried for my daughter who was witnessing her child die in front of her eyes. I felt terrible that Kaitlyn saw her grandma's tears containing the grief that I encased inside me. There wasn't a person to blame for Kaitlyn's brain cancer diagnosis, suffering, and impending death.

I gathered my strength and courage and explained to the doctor that these laws added an extra burden on Elizabeth, who was already stressed and exhausted. She had to ask all the questions and express any concerns. It would make sense that because I was living with Elizabeth and Kaitlyn that I could be allowed to participate in this area and share the communication responsibilities when needed. The solution was obvious and simple. The doctor asked a social worker to provide us with the necessary legal documents to sign so I could legally converse with medical personnel and not break any laws. The papers were placed in Kaitlyn's file, and I kept a set in my possession.

That night Kaitlyn visited me in a dream. She looked like her healthy self, and I was grateful to see the image of the child I recalled so well and profoundly missed. Kaitlyn spoke to me in the voice imbedded in my memory that I longed to hear. "It is best that I die from DIPG. It is no one's fault. It is just how it's supposed to be."

I woke up and checked the room. I looked for Kaitlyn and found her sleeping peacefully nestled under the covers. I sat on my bed and did my morning meditation. I was grateful for the night dream. It started me on a new path that let love and acceptance guide me.

Kaitlyn Gem

Grandma, I hate going to radiation, and I hate not going
to radiation. I need to go to radiation so the bump in my
head will shrink and I can live. Why do I have a bump in
my head? I wish I never got a bump in my head. Grandma,
I love you. You are with me every day, and you are always
there for me and Mommy. You bring my snack and my
medicines. You, Mommy, and me are the best team.

Kaitlyn was a wise and perceptive child. She protested going to the
oncology appointments and radiation treatments and spoke her truth. "I
hate waiting one hundred hours. I want to go home and play with my toys
and you and Mommy."

A Different Life

The standard treatment protocol for children with the **DIPG** diagnosis is radiating the tumor in an effort to shrink the cancerous growth in the brain stem and provide a period of time with less symptoms before the tumor comes back and ends life. We read and inquired about chemotherapy trials that might be considered, but nothing seemed compatible with the goal of quality of life because medicines in the experimental phase had unknown and potentially horrible side effects.

Elizabeth was usually informed by phone calls from the oncology department of dates and times to bring Kaitlyn for the radiation treatments, doctor appointments, blood tests, and other medical interventions. Elizabeth managed to keep track of it all very well. She was told what medicines to give Kaitlyn and the dose and frequency of each drug. Kaitlyn was put on high doses of steroids in anticipation of the radiation treatments. Then she needed antacids, antibiotics, and anti-fungal medicines to prevent possible side effects of the steroids. She was given a variety of pain medicines to help manage her headaches. She was prescribed antipsychotic medications to reduce anxiety, mood swings, and auditory hallucinations. She had medicines to help her cope with nausea and assist with bowel functions and instructions on caring for her chest port.

The medicines were administered by Elizabeth and me several times a day. We kept charts to record doses, so we knew exactly what we gave her and what to administer next. We devoted a table to keep all her medicines in a safe place and at close range. Many of the medicines had to be made child-friendly by us, meaning chopped up, dissolved in liquids, or mixed in applesauce. Kaitlyn was mostly cooperative about taking her medicines, and soon it became an accepted routine in her life. The list of medicines increased, changed, and were modified to adjust to her changing needs.

We were soon emerged in a daily routine that revolved around the care of a child living and dying because a brain tumor invaded her head. I woke up at four o'clock each morning and left in my pajamas to drive to my house to shower, have a quick breakfast, and prepare myself for the day. The streets were empty, and I thought about what I would tell a police officer if I was stopped. Would I cry as I explained the circumstances of my mission? Would the officer cry with me because he knew about loving a child and could empathize with the profound sadness I was feeling?

I returned by six to my girls, still upstairs and sharing a moment together as they prepared to leave for the radiation treatment. Kaitlyn greeted my entrance with a loud, "Hello, Grandma. We are up here. Come see us."

After a few weeks passed, our daily regimen became physically difficult to navigate and psychologically heartbreaking to endure. Kaitlyn evolved into a confused and angry child. Elizabeth carried her down the stairs as Kaitlyn moaned. Kaitlyn was robbed of her childhood and forced to endure scary procedures and bodily pain. We let her guide the conversations as we drove to the hospital and welcomed comments that resembled the child we knew.

"Grandma, there is a pigeon eating cold pizza that is on the ground in the street. Can you believe it? The poor bird is so hungry."

When we left the security of home with Kaitlyn, we felt vulnerable. We perceived that the stares from strangers or heads turning away were judgements that Kaitlyn's appearance was too ugly to tolerate. I thought about when I was a child and was told it was impolite to look at people who were suffering and wondered if that explained these hurtful encounters. Elizabeth and I discussed that a smile with eye contact would provide a moment of care and support with the message, "You are not alone. I recognize that you are in pain. Please allow me to enter your space for a moment and comfort you." A simple gesture would have helped us with the isolation. I stored this lesson and vowed to offer a smile of encouragement and hope the next time I encountered a person in need of a kind human connection.

The radiation treatment required a waiting time that was difficult for the impatient child. Kaitlyn's discomfort was evident as she squirmed in her wheelchair and protested the wait. Elizabeth, Grandpa, and I attempted to entertain her with jokes and stories. Some days Kaitlyn enjoyed people-watching and looked at the men and the women in their hospital gowns walking to get their treatments. I suspect it gave her comfort to know she was not the only person doing this regimen.

Every episode required general anesthesia, radiation, and a recovery period in different parts of the hospital. Following the routine, we walked the long halls of the Cancer Treatment Center to the area where a nurse awaited our arrival. Kaitlyn was not released to go home until tubes were flushed and vital signs were stabilized and recorded. She awoke in pain and confusion, evidenced by her roaring screams and powerful cries. Elizabeth climbed into the bed to offer her comfort and a sense of protection from the frightful ordeal.

There was a nurse we encountered who was consistently sensitive to the situation. She offered love and kindness while performing the medical tasks. Her compassion for Kaitlyn was evident in the soft tone of her voice and her gentle words. She let Kaitlyn direct the tempo of the scene.

"I want to eat my tortilla and cheese first. Then you can flush the tube. Grandma always brings me two cookies for dessert. One cookie is for me, and one cookie is for her. I eat Grandma's cookie because she doesn't like too many sweets, so I help her." Kaitlyn trusted this nurse and shared a little of her heart with her.

The radiation regimen lasted eight weeks. During that time, Kaitlyn gained forty pounds as an aftereffect that resulted from high steroid treatments. The thirty-five-pound child was now trapped inside a seventy-five-pound body. Her lively spirit was negatively affected and changed by psychosis that resulted from medical treatments, radiation, steroids, and DIPG. Kaitlyn was furious and expressed her outrage without reserve. We approached daily routines with as much flexibility as possible. Kaitlyn expressed her misery by screaming, biting, scratching, kicking, and pinching us. She banged her head on the floor and picked at her own skin, causing bruises to her body. Then, sometimes, she sat in removed silence with an occasional grumble or sob. The distant behaviors were the most difficult because we felt removed from her, and it gave us a glimpse into the near future.

Elizabeth and I assisted Kaitlyn as she learned to adjust to her infirmity and her limitations and maintain dignity in the process. We were determined and committed to provide the highest quality of life for Kaitlyn. She now had to live with a malignancy that affected her balance, vision, and limb movements. Her mood swings disrupted her usually positive disposition, causing outbursts and potentially dangerous behaviors. We worked together to calm her mind, so she could successfully engage in activities for her health and enjoyment. My approach used humor to get her attention and guide her away from a thought trapped in negativity. Elizabeth used direct eye contact, motherly touching, and simple words to clearly state the problem and gently guide her to a solution. Our variation in styles gave us options when Kaitlyn's brain, head, and body were overwhelmed with pain and confusion.

We devised original and efficient approaches as we administered medicines, went to appointments, and provided daily body care essentials. I bribed Kaitlyn with an ice cream sundae in her bath if she would cooperate and let us wash her hair. "Grandma, you are very silly," she giggled as I walked into the bathroom carrying the treat.

Elizabeth and I supported each other day and night in an undertaking to earn a Kaitlyn smile, an agreement of cooperation, and a moment of comfort as she suffered from her horrendous torment. When we could achieve an instance of composure, we were profoundly grateful. Sometimes we succeeded with a cookie, a story, a comfortable positioning of her body, or a stronger medicine that sedated her and gave her brief episodes of freedom from painful headaches, auditory hallucinations, and spiritual distress. Sometimes we managed to make a connection with Kaitlyn and her amazing spirit that had temporarily shifted but never disappeared entirely. We accepted these points in time as treasures that nourished each of our souls.

Elizabeth and I never abandoned each other, even when we were exhausted and the circumstances appeared grim and shocking. There was an episode when Kaitlyn refused to put on pajamas and lay in her bed screaming, spitting, and aiming to bite us. She finally exhausted herself and fell asleep, releasing us from this terrible episode of distressing actions. Elizabeth and I contemplated the situation as we watched the child next to us find peace for the moment. Where was Kaitlyn? This child barely resembled the little girl we put to sleep in this bed before cancer took a claim on her.

We were devoted to finding Kaitlyn and helping her achieve serenity. Elizabeth, Kaitlyn, and I had an exceptional bond that unified us as a team and made us stronger than our individual selves.

The Road to Recovery

On Independence Day, we rang the bell. That is the tradition followed by many cancer patients to celebrate the completion of radiation treatments.

Kaitlyn exited this phase of treatment in a state of psychosis, wheelchair dependent, and at her maximum weight of seventy-five pounds. She looked and behaved very differently from the little girl in May who was diagnosed with DIPG. It was difficult to recognize the child from eight weeks prior. She grieved for the loss of her body functions and her clear mind. She sat on the couch and moaned or screamed, not wanting to be touched or spoken to. She did not want to be seen by visitors.

Elizabeth and I believed the strong Kaitlyn spirit was hidden but not gone, and we hoped that she could recover from her grim state of existence. We were determined and committed to helping Kaitlyn achieve the highest quality of life possible. We felt confident that if we worked with her mind, body, and spirit, she could live the rest of her life with gratification, comfort, and joy. We absolutely recognized that it was essential for Kaitlyn to transcend from this grim state and achieve a new aspiration for life. We rejected the notion to just wait for Kaitlyn's life to end.

My work as a speech and language pathologist awarded me years of knowledge about treatment for children with challenging needs. I believed that with a goal and an action plan, we could assist Kaitlyn in regaining the skills needed to walk. Elizabeth and I set into motion our commitment to help Kaitlyn regain her physical strength and endurance. Every day, several times a day, we worked with Kaitlyn to help her obtain physical strength. She was a physically strong child before cancer and its debilitating consequences. I remembered how she could pull herself up the slide at the park, run fast at soccer, and not appear tired after a swimming lesson. We knew we may never see Kaitlyn like that again, but we knew we had to try to help her achieve a state of existence that opened more opportunities for fun and quality of life.

We started out slowly to wake up her muscles and get her strength and confidence back. We requested physical and occupational therapy, and two hours of motor work a week was granted. I watched the experts work with Kaitlyn and used my observations to daily guide her to wake up her legs, arms, and core. I obtained an exercise step and placed it in the middle of the living room. I wanted Kaitlyn to see it and recall the memory of her legs that not too long ago could go up and down a step with ease.

The first time she tried, I used my muscles to lift her safely up and help her down. We both rested on the floor and laughed at Grandma's strong arms. I encouraged Kaitlyn to watch me go up and down the step as I clowned around with this new toy to ignite her memory and entice her to join me in the fun. She caught on to my persistence, and soon it became her achievement. We used creativity and muscle to go up and down the stairs in the house. Results of our work and play came quickly, and we rejoiced as we added other motor fun play.

A friend loaned us a therapy tricycle for Kaitlyn to enjoy riding. Super Grandma moved the furniture in the living room to give Kaitlyn space to ride, laugh, and strengthen her legs. Kaitlyn was moving, laughing, and becoming motivated to do more each day. Her psychosis lifted, and her personality returned. Kaitlyn was proud of her achievements and encouraged friends and family members to witness her perform her regained skills. She was delighted with herself as she reentered the world.

Elizabeth got a kitten for Kaitlyn and she served as an excellent motivator. Kaitlyn crawled around with her to enjoy her baby cat and engage her in fun cat adventures, like fetch the ball and catch the mouse. Kaitlyn's activities resembled a healthy child. She began to lose weight, and body movements were reclaimed and utilized in a natural manner. Kaitlyn did not need us to encourage her to play. Just like a healthy child, she initiated games and activities and invited us to join her. We enjoyed house bowling, performed yoga poses, and danced our way into giggles and fun. Elizabeth and I were thrilled by her progress and physical accomplishments. Her emotional health blossomed too. We were able to enjoy her beautiful sense of humor and loving heart once again.

Kaitlyn looked in the mirror and recognized herself. This brought back her beautiful smile. I glimpsed my granddaughter again, and she was a dazzling sight. Kaitlyn could walk, run, climb, and not be dependent on us pushing her in the wheelchair. We achieved our worthy goal. Her current quality of life gave us hope for a brighter future. We lived in the moment and celebrated each day as a fine gift to treasure.

We rested on the couch and practiced fine motor skills. We painted rocks, colored pictures, played with stickers, and did other various art projects. Mommy and Kaitlyn shared special love moments as they snuggled and created all sorts of masterpieces. Kaitlyn always loved to draw rainbows. We watched her as she concentrated to follow her brain's instructions to draw a perfectly designed rainbow.

I started keeping a journal with Kaitlyn when we first arrived home from the hospital. At first, I directed her to put her hand on my hand as we recorded her feelings and experiences. I thought it would serve to help her process her life events and emotions. Kaitlyn requested writing in her journal daily. We recorded past memories and current events. We drew illustrations of our garden, the zoo, Kaitlyn's preschool, the neighborhood park, and visits with friends. We wrote about feelings of frustration, sadness, and anger that coexisted next to love, joy, and hope. Together, we coauthored a book that brought some meaning to this often confusing existence. When people visited us, Kaitlyn invited them to read her story, so she could share her heart with friends. This diary provided a record of memories from Kaitlyn when she was working on accepting her life as she lived with a tumor in her head, the consequences of radiation and drug treatments, and her recovery leading her to her new normal.

During this time, medicines were reduced and changed. Kaitlyn had a significant decrease in her appetite. She was in a constant state of nausea, and food didn't appeal to her. This forced us to explore alternative means to help her get some relief from this daily discomfort. We researched the use of medical marijuana as a treatment for young patients with similar symptoms. Elizabeth discussed this with the hospice nurse, and she agreed it was worth trying. Elizabeth spent hours completing the necessary paperwork that contained numerous forms to complete. The application was approved, and we received the clearance to purchase medical marijuana drops. We saw immediate results, as Kaitlyn's nausea lessened and she started to enjoy eating again.

This period offered us hope, fun, and encouragement in the here and now—a chance to treasure our time together and rejoice in quality of life.

A Time Out from the Hospital

The radiation treatment was completed, and recovery from treatment was achieved as best as we could ascertain. It's impossible to judge whether it added quality or quantity of life for Kaitlyn. Perhaps she would have experienced a higher quality of life with less suffering if she hadn't had the radiation treatments. Perhaps if she had just received pain and symptom management, she could have avoided the horrible ordeal from a treatment protocol that provided no hope of saving her. I believe doubts are a normal part of the process when witnessing a loved one experience grave suffering.

Kaitlyn received a brain scan approximately four weeks after her radiation was completed. We had observed progress in Kaitlyn's overall condition, and we hoped this would be an indication that the tumor was significantly destroyed, and she could have a longer life span. Kaitlyn's parents were asked to meet with the oncologist to discuss the results. Elizabeth came home with the news that the doctor confirmed that indeed the brain scan showed the tumor had shrunk; however, there was no way to predict how long Kaitlyn would enjoy any quality of life. He encouraged Kaitlyn's parents to have as many fun experiences as possible with her.

Fun was the highlight and goal of every day with Kaitlyn. Enjoying life with friends, family, and each other filled our days with happiness. Each morning we sat with Kaitlyn and let her guide us to plan a day rich with experiences that would bring us all joy and create beautiful memories together.

Kaitlyn Gem

Grandma, it was so great to hear Andy Mason sing at the
library. Did you hear when Andy Mason told everyone in
the library that my name is Kaitlyn? That was so kind of
him. Everyone there now knows my name.

Kaitlyn lived for seven months following her diagnosis of DIPG. Throughout
this entire time, Elizabeth and I strived to enrich her life with friends,
activities, and events designed for her growth and enjoyment. Many people
entered our journey and stayed for the entire duration. I believe we all
benefitted from them opening their hearts and inviting us in.

Kaitlyn Makes Friends

It's almost impossible to believe that a five-year-old child with a tumor in her brain stem could make new friends. When Kaitlyn loved someone, it was completely. She intuitively reached out to people and connected to each individual from her heart and spirit. Most people could not resist her rewards and were drawn to her to receive more offerings. She had an old, wise soul that knew whom to trust, whom to love, and whom to share her treasures with.

Kaitlyn and I saw Andy Mason perform at the Cherry Hills Library during the summer of 2016, when Kaitlyn had just turned four years old and brain cancer was not a reality in our daily lives. She loved his music and child-friendly interactions during the performance. I bought Andy Mason's music CD, and Kaitlyn and I listened to it endlessly in my house and car. We carried it with us, ready to enjoy it anywhere.

Her favorite song was called "Spring Chicken." Kaitlyn sang it with her beautiful four-year-old voice, adding words and body movements to enhance her experience and joy when performing it. She turned it into a ten-minute performance, and I was always happy to hear her sing. Occasionally, I joined in when I had her approval. Kaitlyn sang to anyone who had time to listen and appreciate her musical gift. We listened to the CD in my car on our way to gymnastics, school, swimming lessons, soccer practice, grower's market, Trader Joe's, and other various destinations that filled our days. When the song "Spring Chicken" came on, we were always excited to hear it. Kaitlyn regularly told me in a kind and loving manner, "Grandma, please sing in your head. I want to hear Andy Mason sing the song."

When she was diagnosed with DIPG, I sent an email to Andy introducing myself and telling him about Kaitlyn and her diagnosis. I asked him if he could possibly visit us. I hoped he might have another concert in our neighborhood and would be amenable to my appeal to grant a little girl her dream. Andy responded quickly with a positive comeback, and we set a date for a home concert. He came to the house for a performance the day before Kaitlyn's fifth birthday.

I invited a small group of family and friends to attend this special pre-birthday event. Andy Mason was her favorite singer and soon became her cherished friend. We had a fantastic afternoon listening to him sing, talk, and tell stories. He then settled on the couch next to Kaitlyn, and the man and child quickly became buddies.

I bought two dozen fancy cookies from Whole Foods to add to the festive occasion. Andy asked Kaitlyn to choose the cookies they should eat.

Kaitlyn studied each cookie and described their unique qualities. "This one is huge, this one has chocolate and sprinkles, and this one is shaped like a leaf with green frosting. How many should we eat, Grandma?" Kaitlyn carefully selected the cookies that she believed she and Andy would enjoy.

They whispered and laughed together as new friends usually do when they share cookies and time. We all had a magical occasion when cancer was not dominating. Life was conquering cancer. Love was happening, and we were ecstatic.

It was a valuable moment in time to treasure—an opportunity for Kaitlyn to enjoy being a child with a birthday approaching the next day. Before Andy departed, he offered to return to visit his new friend Kaitlyn soon. His commitment to join our journey was set in stone. He agreed to make an entrance the following week on my birthday. Our plans gave us hope for another celebration of life, and we rejoiced in anticipation of his next visit.

When he got to the house the following week, I opened the door to greet him, and in walked a spring chicken. We all had a tremendous laugh from his funny and ridiculous costume. Elizabeth and I imagined what the neighbors thought as he came to the house in the chicken suit.

Kaitlyn suffered headaches from weeks of radiation and needed extra pain medicine to remain comfortable as she demonstrated her love to her new and dear friend. Andy brought a book for Kaitlyn to enjoy and presented it to her in costume. The friends huddled together with Mommy on the couch as he read to them. Kaitlyn tried to be a good listener with a positive attitude even while in apparent discomfort and pain. Andy agreed to return on Elizabeth's birthday in a month.

I invited Andy to come for a lunch celebration in honor of Kaitlyn's Mommy's special day. Andy Mason arrived as planned. Kaitlyn was suffering immensely from seven long weeks of radiation. She barely spoke to us and appeared consumed by emotional and physical discomfort. Andy sat on the couch next to her and softly read a book to her. He recognized she was distressed and brought a calm and loving manner into her world as he attempted to relieve her suffering with his soothing voice and gentle approach. They were true friends, and their bond was not rattled.

Kaitlyn was agitated and uncomfortable when we ate our lunch. She begged us, "Be quiet! You are hurting my ears."

We sat together and ate in silence, letting her know she was not alone on this horrible journey.

We loved her, and we were with her—always. There was nothing she could do or say that would change our devotion.

After radiation was completed, it took weeks for Kaitlyn to get some strength and motivation to leave the house for a public activity and enter the world outside the security of her home. Andy Mason had a show scheduled at the local library, and I discussed with Kaitlyn and Mommy a plan to attend. Kaitlyn absolutely wanted to be present for the performance. Elizabeth and I set out with Kaitlyn, wheelchair, medicines, and determination to see our friend perform in the same venue we saw him the previous year when cancer only happened in other people. Kaitlyn sat in her wheelchair in front of Andy with a huge smile on her face. She laughed at all his silly jokes, sang along to his tunes, and totally embraced each moment as a child engaged in an experience created just for her enjoyment.

Andy put on his chicken suit in preparation to sing "Spring Chicken." As he got in costume, he told the audience about Kaitlyn and how I had contacted him and shared with him that this was Kaitlyn's favorite song. He refrained from mentioning her illness. He didn't have to because it was probably obvious to many and totally unnecessary to single Kaitlyn out as a sick child. That day, Kaitlyn enjoyed her favorite singer's performance. After the concert, Andy came to our house for lunch, stories, and playtime.

This man devoted time, energy, and love to Kaitlyn. He introduced us to his family, visited Kaitlyn's preschool for a magnificent classroom concert, and sent messages to Kaitlyn on my phone when he couldn't visit. He wanted her to know she was his significant buddy.

Andy visited Kaitlyn a few days before she died. She was very uncomfortable, and yet, she attempted to play with him. She asked me to make matzah ball soup for him and serve chocolate pudding for dessert because she had observed his delight in eating those foods at another visit. She had declared it was his favorite meal.

Andy Mason never knew Kaitlyn before cancer invaded her head. But he knew her well, and they shared a special bond. A few days after Kaitlyn died, Andy visited Elizabeth and me. We looked at pictures of Kaitlyn from all the years of her short life. He got to see what Kaitlyn looked like before DIPG entered her head and took over her physical being. The illness changed her appearance and body form and eventually forced Kaitlyn's spirit to leave her body. Andy witnessed Kaitlyn's final seven months on earth, and during that time, they developed an endless love. He shared with me that he looked for signs of her spirit in rainbows, trees, sunsets, and flowers.

As we looked at pictures of her, we were reminded of the beautiful Kaitlyn who graced us with her physical being and left us, never forgetting her beautiful soul. Elizabeth and I packed some of Kaitlyn's special belongings that we believed Andy and his family would enjoy and Kaitlyn would have chosen for them. We wanted them to have meaningful items that would give them joy, just as they gave us joy during this journey. Kaitlyn would absolutely approve of bestowing some of her treasures to Andy Mason and his family. Her giving heart and love for her friend was deep, true, and beautiful. He was her rock star.

Kaitlyn Gem

Grandma, that was the biggest birthday party I ever went to. Everyone sang "Happy Birthday" to me. Being five years old is wonderful. I knew the small, beautiful cake was for me to take home. I will share it with you and Mommy. I will get the biggest piece. You don't eat a lot of cake because you are already very sweet. So I will help you and eat your dessert.

Kaitlyn was forced to abruptly end her preschool year six weeks before completion because of the onset of brain cancer. The Sunset Mesa School community maintained their commitment, love, and devotion to Kaitlyn during her entire life. The teachers, staff personnel, parents, and students provided us with love and devotion as they demonstrated their support and faithfulness to the child they claimed as one of their own.

A Milestone Birthday

Kaitlyn completed eight months of school as a healthy little girl when her life changed forever. As her birthday approached, her daily life routines were altered in unimaginable ways.

She no longer attended school because she attended radiation treatments to shrink the cancer in her head. Her birthday would happen in spite of the circumstances of her health.

On Kaitlyn's birthday, the preschool coordinated a celebration for her with a school-wide party. She was away from her classmates for a month and would not be able to return for the rest of the school year because of her sickness. On May 22, 2017, the entire school created a day to honor Kaitlyn. Everyone arrived at school that day wearing the shirt designed to celebrate her. It had "Kaitlyn's Pack" printed on the front in big and bold letters. There were two cancer symbols, one in a badge and the other one in a heart. A female dog face was on the shirt, representing Kaitlyn's favorite television show *Paw Patrol*. The shirt captured a piece of Kaitlyn's current life scene.

The preschool director invited us to attend the school on her special day. They were willing to accommodate our time schedule and wait for us to bring Kaitlyn to the party.

We followed our morning routine of administering her medicines, getting the radiation treatment with sedation and recovery time, and heading home for bath, breakfast, and more medications. Elizabeth and I had mixed feelings about going to the school that day. Kaitlyn's physical comfort and moods were unpredictable and getting difficult to remedy away from home when we didn't have access to all of her medicines, a familiar bathroom, and the necessary supplies to care for her.

But it was her birthday and probably her last birthday. And it was a party, and Kaitlyn loved parties. So we put on our Kaitlyn's Pack shirts and went to the school. Everyone at the school greeted us wearing their own Kaitlyn's Pack shirts, and the smiles on their faces reflected the love in their hearts. The shirts were designed and sold as a fundraiser to help Elizabeth with financial expenses. They were worn with pride and love to show support for the person at their school who now lived as a brave child fighting a battle to live a little longer.

The entire school was ready when we arrived and sang "Happy Birthday" to Kaitlyn. She sat in her wheelchair among her friends and delighted in eating a cupcake with her people. There were balloons, presents, and treats—a milestone birthday celebration for Kaitlyn to celebrate her courage and chance to be five years old. Kaitlyn remained quiet as she observed the people and festive surroundings. She beamed a beautiful smile as she looked at her mommy, recognizing the love showered on her that day.

We appreciated that this school devoted a day to celebrate Kaitlyn. It was a true gift of love with a profound message for everyone that Kaitlyn's birth and life were worth a magnificent celebration complete with singing, fun, and cake. The collective school message told us we were not alone on this scary and sad journey. Everyone who was present that day and participated in the Kaitlyn celebration received a gift to treasure and live in their hearts forever.

Their world was enhanced as they cultivated selflessness. I believe the students and adults present that day will remember that there was a huge celebration of life for the little girl at their school who left unexpectedly and too soon. I think they will understand the importance of celebrating each individual as a special life blessing, especially on their birthday.

When Kaitlyn turned five, it was our last chance to celebrate a birthday with her, although we plan to always celebrate Kaitlyn and honor her birthday. I'm grateful that Kaitlyn's school, with all the beautiful children and adults present that day, gave us the incredible gift of the birthday celebration experience and a treasured memory of a special day for her. The beautiful smile she radiated that day is imprinted in my heart and cherished in my mind.

Kaitlyn Gem

Grandma, I'm so happy Ava came to play with me today. I didn't play with her for a long time, and I missed my friend. I took Ava upstairs to my room, and I showed her my jewelry, Buddhas, books, and bed. I told her to try my special way of getting up the stairs. I promise you I was careful and mindful. I sat on my bottom and moved very slowly, just like you and I practiced. Ava sat next to me, and we went up the stairs together. That's what friends do. They join you and go the way you need them to. It was so much fun to sit next to each other and just move up each step, holding hands like partners. It took a long time to get up to the top. We laughed and talked the entire way up to my room, and then we were ready to play.

Kaitlyn and Ava met at preschool, and the girls quickly bonded. They modeled a relationship founded in love and acceptance as they developed a loving friendship. The people who observed them together learned valuable lessons from these two precious children. Elizabeth shared with me her amazement and gratitude that her daughter got to experience the joy of having a best friend.

Kaitlyn's Best Friend

Kaitlyn and Ava met at preschool, and these girls did not waste a moment becoming best friends. Their unique interactions demonstrated a bond of acceptance and commitment. They held hands as they walked on the playground, harmonizing their pace and creating a stride that fit their momentum. They accepted their unique interests and gave each other the space and freedom to explore their own passions. They felt secure in their bond of friendship and trusted they would be back together in time.

After radiation, when Kaitlyn was ready to have a friend come visit, Ava and her mom came to the house for a playdate. I was very concerned that Ava wouldn't recognize Kaitlyn. They had not seen each other in three months, and Kaitlyn looked quite different with the steroid weight gain, haircut, and labored body movements. As soon as Ava walked into the house, the girls hugged and got right down to the business of being friends. The comrades didn't need to discuss looks, weight gain, fears, or plans. They needed to be together. They laughed and played, just as they had before cancer invaded our peace. They accepted each other as true friends do.

This was the first of many happy get-togethers with Ava. It felt amazing to witness these little girls as they shared a bond of friendship that many people don't achieve in a lifetime. We were committed to the value of this special relationship and attempted to endorse and nurture it as frequently as possible. Ava's family required very little notice to meet us at a destination to let the girls enjoy as much time together as possible. We were grateful for episodes that brought joy to the young friends as they created treasured moments for Kaitlyn and lasting memories for Ava.

Kaitlyn Gem

Grandma, I'm ready to go to school. It's a fun place to be. It's so nice that they let you stay. I'm a lucky girl that I can see my Grandma anytime I want. You are the only grandma that stays at my school the whole time with me. They are so kind to give you a bench to sit on, so you can relax and read a book while I go see my friends and have a great time.

Kaitlyn was ready to return to school about two months after radiation was completed. Her chronological age and developmental skills pointed to Kindergarten. Elizabeth felt safety and comfort were the priorities and chose for her to return to the preschool setting that was familiar, inviting, sheltered, and established in an atmosphere of love.

Return to Preschool

Kaitlyn loved learning. She embraced every day with an inquisitive mind, curious nature, and loving attitude. She had an amazing vocabulary and expressed her ideas and concerns about life in a manner beyond her years. One day when I was bringing our lunch outside, I dropped my cup of tea. Kaitlyn exclaimed, "Grandma, the beautiful pottery broke into so many pieces and cannot be fixed. So much work went into making that cup, and it is now gone forever. That is so sad. Please try not to let that happen again."

She loved to play outside on playground equipment and proved herself to be brave and strong. She was willing to follow most of my rules and ready to negotiate the ones she deemed unnecessary or unjust.

"Grandma, if you are cold, go inside the house and watch me from the window. I'll be fine, and I'm really quite comfortable outside."

She attended preschool three days a week when she was four years old. At the beginning of the school year, there was no inclination that this would be her last opportunity to attend school and participate as a student with a strong, healthy body. We didn't know that this year in preschool was her last chance to go to school with a mind free from medications and side effects that hampered her balance and security and undoubtedly presented other challenges that only Kaitlyn knew existed. And we never imagined that Kaitlyn's schooling would end in preschool. She would never go to kindergarten or beyond. When she started school, her only cares concerned playing, learning, and making friends.

Kaitlyn wanted to return to school when the new school year started. She regained important skills like walking, climbing into her car seat, and getting in and out of the car with minimal assistance. The director of the preschool invited Kaitlyn to attend there again. We devised an abbreviated schedule that considered Kaitlyn's unique needs and the classroom routine. The opportunity to go to preschool allowed Kaitlyn to return to the familiar setting she abruptly left in the spring. She could be with the same teachers and many of the kids who already loved her. She could be with her bestie, Ava.

It was like going home to a safe and accepting place. Elizabeth and I were delighted that Kaitlyn was given the opportunity to participate in the autumn activity that all healthy children her age do. I arrived with Kaitlyn and her backpack when she felt well enough to be in a school setting. Kaitlyn was excited and happy to attend preschool for a limited amount of time and be with her classmates in the environment where she'd learned and played as a healthy child just a few months before.

Her first day back was exciting and scary for us. Elizabeth came too, as she was not quite ready to release her child from her motherly care. We stayed close to Kaitlyn, monitoring her every move and rejoicing in this apparent milestone from illness to wellness. Kaitlyn was reserved at first and then relaxed into a comfortable place among the other students.

I was the designated driver and caretaker of Kaitlyn when she went to school. I sat on a bench outside the classroom so she knew I was close by if she needed Grandma love. For several weeks, Kaitlyn got to spend a few hours a day being a student again. Each day we attended, the teachers and children welcomed Kaitlyn with warm greetings and encouragement for Kaitlyn to just be herself. The work did not seem that important to Kaitlyn anymore. This time, preschool was to sit in circle next to the kids, listen to books read by the teachers, play outside with friends, and share her love with comments, kisses, and hugs to anyone ready to receive her generous gifts. Kaitlyn frequently checked on me and blew me kisses or waved to me, knowing I was always there to support her and give her the security she may need if she felt tired or uncomfortable. The staff also visited me and showered me with smiles, hugs, and thoughtful comments that warmed my heart and nurtured my soul. They assured me that Kaitlyn was doing fine and enjoying her time with the kids. I felt supported in this worthy endeavor to promote Kaitlyn's happiness and growth. Preschool was a great place for both of us to spend a few hours engrossed in being a Grandma and a student.

Kaitlyn's prognosis posed an unusual experience for everyone who encountered her presence there. The director assured Elizabeth and me that she informed every parent in Kaitlyn's class of her health, and they were in full agreement that this was her school and the place she was always welcome. They viewed and accepted Kaitlyn as the precious little human she was, not the horrible disease that invaded her body and forced her into being a child with brain cancer. Yet, they also knew she could die at any time.

I was thankful for their brave minds and generous hearts. Each child, their parents, the faculty, and staff personnel got to participate on this life and death journey. I'm sure everyone was impacted by Kaitlyn's positive energy when she was at school and by her absence when she left.

I believe her presence made a profound impact on her classmates. It is my dream that a child Kaitlyn affected will be inspired to grow up and find the cure for DIPG. My mind conceives another child who played next to Kaitlyn becoming a leader in friendship and promotion of world peace. I'm positive the children who stood beside Kaitlyn at her school will love a little deeper or try a little harder to be compassionate and accepting friends. I'm certain that Kaitlyn will have an impact on this world that I have not yet imagined but I'm certain will be grand.

No one could envision or endorse a path for any child to have a fatal outcome at age five. We were mandated into a journey that is everyone's worst nightmare.

All the people who met Kaitlyn will remember her forever as the beautiful, smart, and funny girl who got sick during the school year and returned to school joyful and determined to be their classmate before she had to leave for the final chapter of her life.

Kaitlyn Gem

Grandma, we love going to our favorite store, Trader Joe's. Tell me what we should buy, and I will remember everything you say. You don't even need a shopping list because I have a great memory.

Kaitlyn had a brilliant mind, a compassionate soul, and a beautiful face. She had an excellent memory and recalled experiences and conversations with explicit details. We approached every day as a new adventure. We did the simple tasks with the same enthusiasm as intriguing expeditions. Kaitlyn viewed a trip to the grocery store as an amusing experience. She delighted in her competency when engaging people in conversations, finding the foods she loved to eat, and collecting a lollipop at the end of the Trader Joe's journey.

A Dear Friend

Kaitlyn loved going to Trader Joe's. She had friendly people to talk to, snacks to try, and shopping carts that were just her size. Kaitlyn loved to visit with Jenna, whom I had grown to know from my small chats with her at the store. She referred to Jenna as Grandma's special friend with a loving heart. Jenna expressed her heartbreak to me when Kaitlyn was diagnosed with DIPG and made a sincere offer to help us in any way possible. The opportunity presented itself when Elizabeth made arrangements to get Kaitlyn a hypoallergenic cat that was bred in California. Jenna volunteered to travel there when the kitten was released by the breeder and bring her home to Kaitlyn.

Kaitlyn loved all animals, and cats were her favorite. Elizabeth wanted to give this special gift to her child. Having her own cat would allow Kaitlyn a chance to mother a life. Kaitlyn was not going to grow up, so this kitten would be her chance to have a creative mothering experience. She could know the joy of welcoming a new family member. We spoke about the kitten as we waited for her to be old enough to leave her biological mother. The cat breeder sent us photographs of her, so we would be acquainted with her face and appearance. We studied her picture and considered a suitable title for her. Kaitlyn decided to name her Gray because it was one of her favorite colors and the cat had gray markings on her paws and head. Elizabeth and I thought it was a befitting choice because of the reasons Kaitlyn stated and because the color gray represents brain cancer awareness.

We went on an outing to the pet store to investigate the supplies needed for a new cat family member. Kaitlyn happily participated in this exciting adventure. She studied the huge display of toys and carefully selected the ones she believed a cat and child would enjoy playing with together. Kaitlyn declared she and Elizabeth would be the kitten's two mothers, and I would be her grandma.

Jenna made all the necessary arrangements to fly to California, get Gray, and bring her home to us. On arrival day, she kept us posted with pictures and text messages regarding their travels. We were eager to embrace this new undertaking. Gray would be a magnificent addition in our home, offering a joyous distraction from sickness and sadness.

Jenna arrived with the kitten in hand straight from the airport. Kaitlyn was asleep. When she went to bed, she knew Gray was on her way, and we would wake her upon her arrival. We brought Gray upstairs and woke Kaitlyn so mother and child could meet. Kaitlyn and Gray were both extremely tired and happy.

"Hello, Gray. I am your mommy. I love you very much. Let's sleep now, and we will play in the morning."

It was a beautiful moment to witness and created a forever memory. Gray snuggled next to Kaitlyn in her bed. Kaitlyn was at peace with her baby.

Gray seemed to sense Kaitlyn's needs, difficulties, and moods. The kitty sat in front of Kaitlyn to claim, protect, and love her. Kaitlyn bonded well with the kitten, whom she called her baby. She spoke to Gray with a kind, mother-like tone in her voice to teach, praise, and express affection. Gray always brought a smile to Kaitlyn's face with her playful nature.

Kaitlyn giggled as she described her kitten's adventures. "Gray put her mouse in her food bowl. I guess she likes mouse-flavored food."

We loved having the kitty addition and included her in our everyday home activities. Our team of three became a unique team of four with a feline as its new member.

Jenna continued to give to us with her loving mind and generous heart. When we had a memorial service to honor Kaitlyn after she passed, Jenna baked the cookies for all who came to enjoy and remember our sweet girl. I'm positive Kaitlyn approved of the delicious cookies Jenna baked, filled with kindness, sweetness, and love.

Kaitlyn Gem

Grandma, did you tell Lynna I love the cakes she bakes
for us? They are not too sweet, so they are a little healthy.
I will eat your piece for you.

Kaitlyn and I shared a riddle that I was already too sweet, so I didn't need
to eat a big dessert. Her solution was she would help me eat my cookie,
ice cream, or any kind of treat. Even when she was extremely sick, she
remembered this proclamation and requested that I pass my dessert to
her. Elizabeth related a time when I wasn't in the house, but Kaitlyn still
announced that she got Grandma's dessert. Kaitlyn was a clever child who
loved sweets and knew how to be savvy and adorable as she ate mine.

Long-Time Friends
Become Devoted Friends

I knew Lynna for many years. We were both friends with the dearest person I ever knew who in the past year had died from amyotrophic lateral sclerosis (ALS). Our love for our mutual friend, Peggy, brought us together on many occasions. Lynna contacted me with a genuine offer to help us after she learned about Kaitlyn's diagnosis.

Her visits started with bringing us food once a week after our busy and exhausting day of radiation and doctor appointments. I would send a message to her when we completed our medical sessions. Lynna knew we were hungry and tired and showed up with lunch complete with napkins, plates, and treats that she baked and prepared as a child-friendly picnic.

Kaitlyn noticed Lynna's commitment to us and looked forward to seeing her with her nourishing gifts. "I'm starving. I know Lynna will bring us something healthy and delicious. And I'm positive she will create for me a special treat because she knows kids love dessert."

Lynna's concise lunch visits grew into fabulous occasions. Kaitlyn and Lynna developed a friendship, and soon, activities blossomed. Lynna brought a huge bag of children's books and stayed to read to Kaitlyn.

Kaitlyn asked, "How many books will you read to me today?"

If Lynna said, "Let's read three books today," then Kaitlyn replied, "I think we should read five books today."

Kaitlyn loved to set the terms and get her way. Her life was confusing and difficult, so these small victories meant an opportunity for her to claim a bit of order and control. It also carved out a block of time to be engrossed in a story with her friend, proving her life could still have meaning and fun. They sat close together on the couch and enjoyed each story, illustration, and discussion. Kaitlyn loved being read to since she was a small child and this activity was a winner. Their mutual laughs and animated conversations could be heard throughout the house and filled our hearts with merriment. The brief visits became occasions of many joyous hours. There were tons of books to read, and no time to waste.

Lynna gave Kaitlyn the book *The Kissing Hand* by Audrey Penn. It became Kaitlyn's theme to share as her end of life was getting closer. She was determined to kiss the hands of the people she loved so they could bring their hands to their hearts and carry her love with them forever.

Bob, Lynna's husband, brought the lunch if Lynna was delayed or had another appointment. Kaitlyn and Bob quickly bonded, and she absolutely enjoyed demonstrating to him her many talents and tricks.

Kaitlyn eagerly shouted, "Bob, look at me ride my special bike in the house and go superfast. I can make a U-turn smoothly in this tight space."

Lynna told Kaitlyn that Bob loved cats. Kaitlyn enthusiastically invited Bob to play with her and Gray and instructed him, "Throw the mouse, and Gray will retrieve it just like a dog." Kaitlyn delighted in playtime with Bob and boasting about her cat's unique fetching talent.

A week before Kaitlyn died, she requested that I bring the waffle blocks from my house to her home because she was positive Bob would enjoy playing with her and this special toy. She was in obvious discomfort that day, but she was determined to have an outstanding experience with her friend. Kaitlyn and Bob created a structure with the blocks and, when doing so, created a bond that sealed their love.

Kaitlyn told Bob, "You are very good at building, and I am too. We made a magnificent creation. It's huge and interesting."

Bob and Lynna were two friends that Kaitlyn made while sick and suffering from pain and side effects of medications. Kaitlyn knew how to bond, connect, and enjoy people. She was an inspiration to watch. She performed a love magic. I extend sincere gratitude to Bob and Lynna as they demonstrated courage, love, and devotion to us on this journey. We all knew the ending of this story, and they never wavered from forming a lifetime connection with my granddaughter. They observed and felt the special nature of this child. Kaitlyn demonstrated how easy it was to live in the moment, connect with people you love, and form a forever bond. I believe Kaitlyn made an imprint on their hearts, so she would never be forgotten by these friends.

Kaitlyn Gem

Grandma, if you are sad, make a cup of tea and drink it
slowly so you can taste the flavors. If you are super sad,
have a cookie with it.

I knew the time was approaching when the physical bond I treasured with
Kaitlyn would cease. I devoted every day as a celebration of her life since
she was born. I contemplated life without her and sometimes found myself
trapped in grim thoughts. Her fatal diagnosis intensified my commitment
to honor her life.

I have imprinted on my soul her smile, laugh, and wisdom. There
were times when my mind was invaded with sadness and misery.
Kaitlyn shared her wise words of advice: "Grandma, when you are
missing me, remember I live in your heart. You can always find me
there. And enjoy your cup of tea. It is healthy and delicious. It's your
favorite drink."

Kaitlyn was mindful and considerate. She took care of me as I cared
for her. Her thoughtfulness and love were always present but seemed to be
heightened as she lived with an illness that drew her closer to death.

When I struggle to live in the moment and find myself borrowing
misery from the past or future, I recall her wise instructions and slowly
drink a cup of tea and nibble on a cookie.

This child enriched my life and helped me understand the blessings of being a grandmother. I am grateful she taught me the simplicity of healing. Her wise, old soul bestowed upon me the enlightened remedy for taking care of deep sorrow and turning it into gratitude and love.

A New and Treasured
Friendship

I made an appointment to visit Sunil Pai, MD, an internationally known expert in integrative medicine, soon after Kaitlyn completed her radiation treatments. His wellness center, the House of Sanjevani Integrative Medicine Clinic, was a place I'd heard about and was eager to enter. I was determined to find a medical professional who could work with Elizabeth and me to help Kaitlyn recover from the side effects of the radiation treatments and better cope with the brain cancer that resided in her head. I wanted Kaitlyn to live with the quality of life she deserved. I always trusted that a holistic medical approach had great value because of its focus on the unique needs of an individual and the stoplight on wellness.

My first meeting with Dr. Pai took place after a brief phone encounter when I related Kaitlyn's diagnosis and current condition. He spent many hours listening to my love, hopes, and description of Kaitlyn's current state of being. He then took the time to discuss and explain a treatment plan that may enhance Kaitlyn's quality of life. He made suggestions for supplements, nutrition, bodywork, massage, pain management, and overall comfort. He endorsed our loving-team approach and appeared grateful to be invited to be a member of our pack.

I told Kaitlyn about my meeting with Dr. Pai and showed her a photograph of the doctor. She studied the picture of his face and declared, "I love this man, and I want to meet him."

Elizabeth and I brought Kaitlyn to meet Dr. Pai and visit him at his office. They immediately bonded with each other as they appeared to share a special connection. Notably, they were both dressed alike that day, wearing plaid shirts and huge smiles. They kneeled next to each other on the floor and pet the office dog. They started a beautiful friendship that moment with a connection that bonded them forever.

Kaitlyn believed she would benefit from Dr. Pai's suggestions and that he would help her achieve a state of wellness. She readily took his suggested supplements to alleviate the head pain and other physical and psychological discomforts. His flexible, diverse, and inclusive doctoring helped her achieve an improved sense of wholeness.

Kaitlyn often asked me to take her to visit her special friend. Every person who worked at the House of Sanjevani welcomed us and made us feel like family members complete with hugs, smiles, kisses, and acceptance. The people in his office appreciated our mission and treated Kaitlyn, Elizabeth, and me with respect and kindness. We felt welcomed and honored as people on a quest together. We didn't need an appointment. We frequented the House to pick up supplements, pet the dog, give updates on Kaitlyn's health, and see Dr. Pai.

Kaitlyn was fascinated with the beautiful wall hangings decorating the environment. She felt inspired to comment and touch each unique display. Everyone there smiled with delight as she expressed her art appreciation. "That is a huge picture on the wall. It's a beautiful scene. It is lovely. I could look at it all day. Grandma, sit with me and enjoy the beautiful picture hanging in front of us."

Dr. Pai consistently regarded us as people who warranted his respect, love, and kindness. He always treated Kaitlyn as a valued person with a beautiful spirit. Elizabeth and I recognized that his suggestions and friendship contributed to her increased happiness. We were grateful for his kindness and medical support. Kaitlyn received the beneficial care that enhanced her quality of life with the bonus of a special friend.

Unfortunately, the cancer was fierce and determined to grow. Our greatest efforts and finest intentions could only keep it at bay for a few months. We were warned that DIPG was a relentless monster and that no child was ever released from its dreadful clutches.

In November 2017, I notified Dr. Pai that Kaitlyn was declining. We made plans for him to visit Kaitlyn at the house. On the morning just before his arrival, Kaitlyn requested a much-needed bath. She no longer enjoyed baths and insisted that her baths were quick and infrequent. She usually cried during the uncomfortable ordeal. But today was different because her special friend was on his way to see her, and she wanted to look and smell good for the occasion.

"Grandma, please help me get dressed in some new clothes today. Comb my hair, so I will be ready to visit with Dr. Pai."

Kaitlyn was happy to greet Dr. Pai as they sat together on the couch and enjoyed being in each other's company. They looked into each other's eyes and connected on a level only they understood. It truly was a unique and beautiful image to witness.

Dr. Pai brought Kaitlyn a huge penguin stuffed animal. He asked her what she would name her new gift. Kaitlyn thought about it for several moments. She usually didn't name toys because, as she explained it, "A toy is not real, so it doesn't need a name. I just call it what it is. And some toys already have names." When she was very young, she renamed a beloved stuffed animal that her parents called Sleepy Bear to Apple. Kaitlyn agreed to give the penguin a name because her friend asked her about it, and she believed it was important to him. She named it Winnie Pie. She was proud of her clever creation.

Before the visit concluded, Kaitlyn took Dr. Pai's hand and kissed him, saying, "Put your hand to your heart, so my love will live in your heart forever." She internalized this concept from the book she recently received called *The Kissing Hand* by Audrey Penn. She embraced the animation of the story as she gave her love to her treasured friend.

Kaitlyn performed this act as her final gesture with many family members and friends who visited during her last days as a gift for all to cherish forever.

Kaitlyn Gem

Grandma, Dr. Pai is a great man. He loves me and helps me, and I love him. He has a peaceful face, a big smile, and a soft voice. I am so glad you found him. He is my forever friend. I hope he comes to visit me again. The penguin he gave me is huge. It reminds me of Dr. Pai's big, loving heart. I named it Winnie Pie. Winnie is for his dog, and Pie is for Dr. Pai. It's a special gift from a special man.

Kaitlyn and Dr. Pai shared a connection that was beautiful to witness.

Goodbye, Friend

I called Dr. Pai a few days after his visit with Kaitlyn to let him know the drastic change of her condition. The hospice nurse told us Kaitlyn was approaching the end of her life. The medicines she received in her port put her in a medically induced coma and relieved her from her pain. Her breathing was peaceful, and she looked beautiful, resting in a serene sleep. Dr. Pai asked if he could visit. I agreed that a visit would be appropriate and appreciated. I shared with him that Kaitlyn hoped she would see him again.

Shortly after we spoke, he arrived, and Kaitlyn opened her eyes, acknowledging the arrival of her dear friend. She came out of the coma and said in her labored breath, "Hello, Dr. Pai. You are here with me. I am happy to see you."

The hospice nurse witnessed this scene and shared her shock and amazement. "I've never seen anyone free themselves from a medically induced coma."

I knew Kaitlyn had a strong will and everlasting bond with this man. They were friends for life and beyond. We held hands and listened to Kaitlyn's favorite meditation about sleeping with the angels, as we shared a final moment of peace and joy together. Dr. Pai and Kaitlyn locked eyes on each other and shared a knowing gaze before he left the room. They said a final goodbye approximately one hour before Kaitlyn left us.

Kaitlyn Gem

Grandma, I know how to make no more strangers. Just talk to people. First say to them your name, and then ask them their name. Then tell them something wonderful about the world. After you share with them, they are your new friend. And that's how you do it. Just speak to someone, and they will never be a stranger again.

Regardless of the weather, Kaitlyn and I walked to the park as often as possible. Kaitlyn loved nature and enjoyed seeing all the treasures in her environment. She delighted in watching bugs crawl, flowers bloom, and leaves change with the seasons. And Kaitlyn loved people. Most people found her endearing and would engage with her in a simple conversation, which she initiated. Kaitlyn's observations about people were simple and true. She lived and loved in the moment. She embraced life with a generous heart and the wisdom of an old soul. She lived by commandments that came naturally to her. I was blessed to hear them as they formulated from her mind into words as she shared and declared her gems to me.

Our Chosen Sister

Julie accepted the role of the ever-present friend, ready to rescue us with gifts for fun, meals for nourishment, and smiles for encouragement to face another day. Her generous deeds flood my memory, as there are too many to recall, acknowledge, and report. Her giving was natural and unpretentious. She was the person we counted on for incidentals we needed or couldn't predict.

Julie frequently arrived at our house with fascinating books, intriguing toys, and fun activities that brought laughter and joy into our world. She always showed up with a smile on her face and a contagious laugh that sprinkled moments of happiness upon our space. She didn't make any demands on us, except to receive the generous offerings she brought and to know they were given with kindness and love. Julie did not expect recognition or praise for her presence. She developed into the loving mother, sister, and friend we needed. She stepped onto this runaway train, apprised of the destination, yet willing to expose her heart and soul to the outcome.

Julie's friendship gave Elizabeth opportunities to briefly leave her surroundings and renew her exhausted self. Sometimes they stood in front of the house chatting and enjoying the moment of each other's company.

Kaitlyn loved hearing her mother's voice. "Mommy, I hear you outside talking to Julie." It comforted her to know her mom was just a few steps away.

Julie seemed to have a keen sense of timing. I recall her bringing the instructions and all the materials necessary to create slime. She looked at Kaitlyn and declared, "I brought something I think you will like, but you may have to persuade your grandma to like it too."

We laughed at the image that the creation of slime brought to our minds. I was hesitant about this present because I imagined it would be more work than fun. I perceived a messy activity full of cleanup and regret. After a few days, I reluctantly encouraged Kaitlyn to help me make the slime that was clearly out of my comfort zone. We played with our new sticky and silly creation as we harmonized our giggles and gladness with this new adventure.

Kaitlyn joyfully laughed as she declared, "Slime is fun." I agreed.

It's a courageous soul who willingly steps on the path that is heading to mournfulness. Elizabeth and I were a solid team, so our bond and choice to service Kaitlyn and each other was never doubted. I was disheartened by the people who quickly exited our lives. They made promises they couldn't honor during this time of need. They were unwilling to grasp the magnitude of the suffering we were experiencing. Friendship is comfortable when the living is easy, but true friends are revealed during a train wreck.

And then there were the people like Julie—the souls who silently pledged their devotion to stay and help and never boasted about the helping hand they delivered. Their actions proved their faithfulness. They made no judgements and carried no demands. They got on the train and rode with us, coping with the bumpy starts and stops. They knew that fatigue and despair influenced our frame of mind and behaviors, and they forgave us, loved us, and accepted the path with us. These people inspirited my view of humanness. They convinced me that life is worth living even when feeling despondent. They demonstrated that joy and sadness are always present and that we need each other to live life completely. How do I thank the people who stayed and proved that leaving was never an option? I believe that the best part about a person like Julie is that my thanks was never required and my gratitude was always understood.

Kaitlyn Gem

Grandma, you are loving and kind. You want everyone to
be healthy, and that's why you make bone broth. Thank
you for making all our lunches so lovely and delicious.
Today you made a mistake. You gave Vicky two pieces of
Swiss cheese, and you only gave me one piece. It's okay,
and I forgive you. I do want another piece of cheese, please.

Kaitlyn lived seventeen days after this visit with Vicky, and it was their
last opportunity to be together. Kaitlyn struggled with pain and physical
limitations; however, her awareness of people, surroundings, and events
remained forever intact.

She was a child who understood life concepts beyond her years. She
had an excellent memory and processed information accurately with her
keen mind and fair judgement. She spoke her truth with a sensitive nature.

A Devoted Friend

Many times Vicky came from Virginia to help in any way possible with Kaitlyn's care and to nurture a relationship with Kaitlyn while there was still time to do so. When Kaitlyn was not well enough for visitors, Vicky sat in another room to be available to go on errands, buy us groceries, and just be present to give us love and support. When Kaitlyn was capable of receiving visitors, Vicky joined us with her gifts of love, food, and friendship. She spoke to Kaitlyn in a voice that contained a sincere message of interest and always gave Kaitlyn the time to respond and be heard. Vicky was willing to enter into a little girl's world that was limited and limitless.

On one occasion, we watched Kaitlyn's favorite movie, *Moana*, together. Kaitlyn sang the songs and periodically warned Vicky about the upcoming scenes, "Vicky, this part is a little scary, but not too scary. I've watched it many times, and I'm a kid, so I think you will be all right."

Kaitlyn was an expert in engaging people, living in the moment, and celebrating life. Communicating with a person was on the top of her list of priorities. She genuinely loved people and readily accepted their gifts, talents, and love. I noticed Kaitlyn become freer with her comments, opinions, and wisdom, as her life was coming to an end. We didn't get to finish the movie that day because Kaitlyn was getting tired and ready to see her Mommy.

A few days after Kaitlyn died, Vicky shared with me that as a special tribute to Kaitlyn, she watched the movie *Moana* and recalled Kaitlyn's singing, her kind and sincere warnings of the scary parts, and her wise grasp of the movie's message. She recalled when Kaitlyn proudly announced, "The girl in this movie is beautiful, smart, and brave." It was a special event we shared with Kaitlyn—a treasured visit when my granddaughter was able to transcend beyond her physical discomforts and enjoy a meaningful experience in her life.

A few weeks after Kaitlyn's final departure, Vicky returned to visit and take her friend Terry, Elizabeth, and me away for a weekend at a nearby resort to help us begin the healing process. Our time away gave us an opportunity to honor Kaitlyn's life as we shared with our dear and loving friends the intimacies residing in our hearts. We shared meals, activities, and tears as we engaged in stories about Kaitlyn and the days surrounding her death. We began the healing process necessary after losing a love so profound and pure. We had a chance to think about Kaitlyn and reminisce about our newly departed little person. We celebrated Kaitlyn's life as we looked back at the child we loved so deeply and intensely.

We were reminded she was loved by so many people, and this truth filled us with a needed tenderness during this surreal time. We were surprisingly calm and able to enjoy food, friends, and conversations during the post-death experience. We loved and accepted Kaitlyn as a priceless treasure and were stunned that we were still alive after Kaitlyn's heart stopped beating. Yet we smiled and enjoyed each other in the beautiful environment that had a backdrop of solid mountains and vast blue skies. Nature and friends were there to assist us as we walked around with broken hearts.

We understood we would experience deep grief and had no clue how it would feel or present itself until it happened. I saw a friend at the supermarket prior to our departure on this trip. Her voice was filled with surprise as she exclaimed, "Leslie, you are walking in the store." My mind repeated that comment many times like a recording I needed to pay attention to. I truthfully didn't know what to expect after Kaitlyn died.

I first met death as a child when my grandfather died. He was a nice old man, and the thought of never seeing him again brought tears to my eyes. I never forgot him. I understood that death was a natural occurrence at the end of a person's life and accepted his passing without too much heartbreak. My parents died when I was a young woman starting my own family. My grief was deep but distracted with the joys and needs of my own children. I made time to cry and felt the pain of becoming an adult orphan. Holidays and special events filled me with memories of my parents and sometimes still do. But isn't that the normal order of life? I accepted and integrated my parents' passing as a natural part of the life cycle and achieved a peace with it.

The recent death of my dear friend Peggy was like a blow to my core and caused me great emotional pain. She was my peer. We were supposed to grow old together as friends. There was nothing natural about her passing. She developed a grave illness that caused her to suffer for years, and death released her from her pain.

Kaitlyn's passing was unnatural, and it released her from pain. But she was a child, and it went against my rules of life. I contemplated my emotions walking among the trees with my daughter and experienced a deep sense of calm along with my sadness. Just three weeks ago I held Kaitlyn's hand and watched her take freedom from a body that was no longer viable. Her pain was over, and her life was completed.

During that weekend, I felt unconditional love for my daughter and my friends. Vicky's generous gifts aided my transition into the grieving process. I devised a simple and profound direction for dealing with my grief. I made a commitment to pair my sad thoughts with positive reflections. When my brain told me how unbelievable and tragic it was that Kaitlyn died, my heart intervened with the reminder that she lived five years by my side, providing love and joy every day. As I longed for Kaitlyn and cried about never having the opportunity to hold her again, I was grateful that I had no sorrow regarding how I took care of her because I always approached each day with her filled with generosity, love, and kindness.

When I considered the final seven months of Kaitlyn life, I was grateful for not having any remorse about the time I devoted to Kaitlyn and Elizabeth. I loved them genuinely and completely. I strived every day to achieve the quality of life we all deserved. We lived with the knowledge that our time together was limited and sacred. We treasured each other as we lived under an umbrella of impending tragedy and profound love.

I concluded that I was blessed to have Kaitlyn in my life for five glorious years. That weekend I began my grieving process in an atmosphere that highlighted Kaitlyn and imbedded the message to me that deep pain and profound love are partners.

Kaitlyn Gem

Grandma, you have many wonderful friends. Your friends are my friends too. They love you and me the same. Sometimes I think they love me a little bit more because your friends always bring me thoughtful presents. I will share the gifts with you and Mommy.

There were so many people willing to join us on this life journey and support us with our growing emotional needs and physical exhaustion. I want to acknowledge them all and thank them from the depth of my soul. I know they gave to us because they felt the calling to serve and grew from the opportunity to help us. Their constant support lifted me when I was tired and carried me when I felt weak or overwhelmed. My community of friends fed my soul.

My Friends Are
Kaitlyn's Friends

My friends knew that Kaitlyn and I shared a special bond. I invited people to join us and help create special moments to enrich Kaitlyn's current life. I also wanted to create vivid memories that I could recapture with an individual in the future when Kaitlyn's physical existence transformed into a memory. People regularly came to witness, participate, and enjoy some festive moments with my constant companion and me.

My friend Jean visited us from out of town and offered to bring a winner kid's meal for lunch. Jean was aware of Kaitlyn's connection to food and wanted to bring refreshments we would relish together. I told her Kaitlyn's favorite food was an organic rotisserie chicken. That was her happy meal.

Jean arrived carrying shopping bags filled with treats. Kaitlyn delighted in the smells and gleefully told Jean that chicken was the best. She enthusiastically thanked Jean for the lunch gift.

As Kaitlyn eagerly helped me empty the bags to discover the many goodies, she announced, "Grandma will cut up the chicken with a sharp knife that I can't touch because I'm a kid. She will put the bones in the crock pot with lots of water to make bone broth all night. Tomorrow we will eat it, and it's very delicious and healthy."

We had a lovely lunch. I washed the dishes and gave Kaitlyn and Jean a chance to experience precious time together. I glanced over and saw Kaitlyn intrigued as she looked at Jean with her wide eyes and listened to a story created just for her enjoyment. Jean expanded the myth to satisfy Kaitlyn's inquisitive mind when she asked questions and made comments that demonstrated she was completely immersed in the tale.

Kaitlyn inquired, "What did the girl say when she saw her things broken? Did she cry? Was she angry? Did she forgive them?"

The visit was a special event for us. I watched as Kaitlyn and Jean connected and the moments flowed with delicious food, an interesting narrative, and a shared experience that was engraved in our hearts. Jean told me she will always remember Kaitlyn as my beautiful granddaughter who loved to eat healthy and delicious food and was fascinated by an enchanting story. Kaitlyn was the child whose blue eyes grew wider with wonder as the storyteller wove a fascinating fantasy for a five-year-old child to savor and enjoy.

Kaitlyn Gem

Grandma, is Papa coming to our house tonight? Last night I taught him how to play with the train set my way. He thought all the tracks needed to be connected for the train to go on it and for us to play correctly. I showed him we just need to have a great time. The tracks don't have to all be connected. It's all about using your imagination, playing together, and having fun. It's not about making the perfect train track. I can't wait to see Papa and play with the trains tonight. We love to have fun together.

Kaitlyn learned rules and used her intelligence and creative mind to justify changing guidelines. She was not shy and perceived herself as capable and correct. We often thought she would become a fantastic lawyer because of her persistence in conveying her message and her inventive argumentative skills.

Kaitlyn's Papa

Kaitlyn called her maternal grandfather Papa. I call him Jerry, and Elizabeth calls him Dad. When Kaitlyn was younger and came to my house, she would ask me in a voice only reserved for him, "Is Papa home?" Her question revealed her deep love and connection to her grandfather. Even if she only got to spend a few minutes with him, it was enough to fill them with joy and create a love moment that would hold them until the next time they saw each other.

Jerry loved when Kaitlyn was at our house on weekends so they could play games, walk to the park, or be in the backyard. They frequently did outside chores together. Watering the plants with each other was a favorite. Kaitlyn created imaginative play activities, and Papa was a happy and willing participant. As he sat in a chair on the lawn, she drove him to various places like California, New York, or the moon.

Walking together to the park was another favorite. Kaitlyn used her park time with Papa to break some of the Grandma park rules. Kaitlyn would confess this to me on her return home, and I would have to reconsider the necessity of my restrictions. Usually, my rules were firm in order to protect Kaitlyn. It seems ironic that safety and health were a priority but no match for this child's fate.

Papa was with us in April when Kaitlyn was diagnosed with DIPG. He was with us when she took her last breath. He was there to pick out the cemetery plot, and he was there for her burial. He drove us to every doctor's appointment and radiation treatment. He visited Kaitlyn after his workday was completed every day. Papa danced around the living room to distract us from pain and give us an opportunity to laugh and forget for a moment our new normal.

Kaitlyn smiled as she affirmed, "Papa is a funny man. He dances like a preschool boy with his arms swinging. He likes to make us laugh."

Papa and Kaitlyn shared a love bond that can only exist between a grandfather and his granddaughter. Papa would do anything for Kaitlyn, and she completely believed it. They both flourished in their special connection. His broken heart was evident as he knew the sweet Kaitlyn voice calling out to Papa would soon be just a memory.

Kaitlyn Gem

Grandma, I love the Play-Doh toy Uncle Jason brought
me. It was so kind of him to have lunch with us and bring
me a special present. He truly loves me, and I truly love
him too. I remember when you said that when Uncle Jason
was a little boy, he and I were like the same person. We
both loved to eat, play, run fast, and laugh. We will always
be alike, loving to have fun every day.

Kaitlyn enjoyed the people in her life fully. She cherished the presents she
received because it connected her to the giver. Toys that required her to
use her imagination and be engaged with another person were her favorite.
She rarely wanted to play alone. The toys or games served as instruments
to have meaningful experiences with people.

Kaitlyn treasured her bond with her Uncle Jason. He was the man who
showed up with toys and smiles. He was the uncle who showered her with
unconditional love and a person her grandma compared her to because
the likeness of their grand spirits shined brightly in the world.

An Uncle to Love

Kaitlyn called my son Uncle Jason. He enjoyed playing with Kaitlyn, and she loved having an uncle who adored her. Watching them interact was a joyful sight, as they shared a connection created in devotion. Their play together usually involved running and laughing. They would spring into action together playing chase or race.

Jason and his soon-to-be bride changed the date of the wedding from December to July with the hope that Kaitlyn would be able to attend their special event. We all were aware of the truth that Kaitlyn's life expectancy was going to be radically reduced, and special occasions needed to be in the now. The wedding date change was a blessing, as Kaitlyn died eleven days prior to the original scheduled plan. Arrangements and adjustments were quickly organized to accommodate the urgency of our new world where time was not in our favor.

The wedding date was set five days after Kaitlyn completed her radiation treatment and three months after her diagnosis. Kaitlyn sat in the front row in her wheelchair to witness a beautiful outdoor wedding ceremony. She wore a gold-and-white dress and dazzling rose-gold shoes for the special day. A wide-brimmed hat added the final touch to her lovely outfit.

Our friend Lea, a hairdresser, came to the house that morning to fix our hair. Lea was a regular at our house, cutting Kaitlyn's hair as we needed to prepare for radiation treatments, school, and now a wedding.

Kaitlyn resisted haircuts but would be draw into Lea's persuasive and loving manner. Lea also brought Kaitlyn a special headband to wear for the occasion, and Kaitlyn agreed it was a lovely accessory to her outfit.

Kaitlyn looked into the mirror and decided, "I don't really look like me. But I am still beautiful."

Kaitlyn was present when her Uncle Jason became a married man. She got to witness the ceremony and go to the wedding reception. She rejoiced as she shared four pieces of wedding cake with me. She was mostly a quiet observer at this event. It was a bittersweet time for Kaitlyn. She expressed her delight to be present at the event but was quite impaired during this time. She could barely walk, and sitting was uncomfortable. She frequently needed help to be adjusted in her chair, as her body just couldn't get comfortable.

It was appropriate to have Kaitlyn present for the wedding of her beloved Uncle Jason. Her absence would have produced a tremendous amount of sadness and pain to all. She was a vital member of our family, and her company was essential. Kaitlyn was there to bring the love she felt for the man who had loved her since she was born.

The photographs of that day show a niece looking very different from the child who used to run around and giggle with her uncle as they shared fun times together. But the pictures portrayed a niece present for her uncle as she loved him and wished to be a part of his special day in July. The snapshots represent a chapter in Kaitlyn's life that was part of our family story.

I felt sad that the family and friends who gathered for the wedding only got to view Kaitlyn from a lens that focused on her illness and not the amazing child that resided in her ill-fated body. In my mind's eye, I envisioned Kaitlyn enjoying the wedding celebration as the spunky child I remembered from just months before as she joyfully played with Uncle Jason. My son and granddaughter were two people who loved parties, people, food, and each other. I am forced to look beyond the physical pictures and recall the joy present on that special day, as family and friends gathered to celebrate life and love. I am grateful Kaitlyn was with me to enjoy a wedding and eat the delicious cakes that symbolized happiness and celebration of life. Kaitlyn being there was a sweet addition to the beginning of her Uncle Jason's new life chapter.

Kaitlyn Gem

Grandma, I chose a great mommy. She is loving and kind and really cares about me and other people. She does important work taking care of sick people and helping them get better. She works hard so we can have a lovely house, great food, and beautiful things.

I love my mommy to infinity. Actually, I love my mommy two infinities.

Kaitlyn enjoyed learning new concepts and verbalizing words that are usually reserved for older children. She was fascinated by mathematical concepts, and the number infinity intrigued her.

She felt her mother's love and devotion completely, and she absolutely loved her mommy two infinities. Her mother loved her two infinities too.

Kaitlyn's Mommy
Is My Daughter

Elizabeth and Kaitlyn shared a bond that was deep, profound, and cast in love from the start. Kaitlyn always said when she grew up she was going to marry Mommy. Kaitlyn also reported that she and Mommy would work together, live together, and take care of each other forever.

Elizabeth was proud to be Kaitlyn's mother. This beautiful child frequently challenged Elizabeth to be patient, creative, and accepting of her child's unique interests and demanding ambitions. Kaitlyn could be persistent and determined when asserting herself and forcing Elizabeth to make split-second decisions on how to accommodate her clever and willful child. Kaitlyn could be profound in her observations about people and life situations. She had the wisdom of an old soul and the playful, adventurous spirit of a young child. She could be unpredictable in her behaviors, yet as thoughtful and considerate as an enlightened human. Her advanced vocabulary added to the intensity of her reasoning powers.

When Kaitlyn was experiencing extremely difficult symptoms from her illness, she looked at her mother and asked, "Will you be okay when I die? I don't know how much longer I can live in this body."

Kaitlyn invited urgent and important discussions to be exchanged that usually do not occur between a young child and her mother. Other times,

Kaitlyn behaved like a preposterous kid. Elizabeth smiled as she related a story about her precocious Kaitlyn throwing herself on the floor of Trader Joe's because she wouldn't allow her to eat rum cake. Kaitlyn screamed, "I love rum cake. It's delicious. I want it. Let me have it!" Elizabeth had to carry Kaitlyn out of the store, leaving groceries and rum cake to be a discussion at home in a calm manner.

I was with them at the nature center when Kaitlyn insisted on getting too close for a mother's comfort to the river's edge. Elizabeth held tight to protect her brave child from the dangers of the water and the unpredictable forces of Mother Nature. Kaitlyn fought her with determination to do what she wanted as she disregarded the potentially dangerous situation. She relied on her mother's protection when childish impulses clouded her thoughtful mind.

These two females shared mother-and-daughter time living as unique roommates in a lovely home together. They took care of each other in a profoundly nurturing manner. The young child and the young professional woman shared a bond of love that was deep and beautiful to witness.

I delighted in the kind and the heartfelt way they interacted together. They were like a unique duo choreographed with rhythm and dancing their beauty. Before Kaitlyn left her body, she reached her arm up to touch her mother's face with her hand. It was a moment frozen in time. It was the last chance for Elizabeth to be physically touched by her precious baby. The child who once lived inside her body now had to live in her heart. Their bond transcends the physical. Kaitlyn invited Elizabeth to acknowledge and embrace the spirit.

My daughter, who always prided herself on being a scientist, opened her heart and mind to acknowledge soul essence so she could continue the love connection she created with her daughter. Her child taught her the divine gift of having a soul. If this was Kaitlyn's mission in the physical world, she did a perfect job. Kaitlyn's life was over in five years; however, her impact of love and spiritual growth was profoundly felt by so many people and changed Elizabeth forever. They must now transcend their relationship, as one lives in the physical world and one lives in the spirit world. They are forever bound and pledged to each other. Their love continues and grows.

Kaitlyn always said she picked Elizabeth to be her mommy. The two wise and beautiful souls were united forever. I was fortunate to be mother and grandmother to these amazing people on this life journey. Elizabeth always intuitively honored each person's spiritual nature, but Kaitlyn gave her permission to openly declare it as an intrinsic part of every living entity.

Elizabeth divulged to me during this heartbreaking path that having five years with Kaitlyn was a gift beyond measure and a treasure to behold forever. My child and grandchild behaved with dignity, courage, and love as they secured their everlasting bond. The sadness may be overwhelming; however, the love continues in a deep and intense kinship that could never be severed.

Kaitlyn Gem

Grandma, your Buddha statues are beautiful. They make
me think about my friend the Dalai Lama. He is a happy
man. His laugh sounds like a song, and his whole body
sings with him. Let's put the Buddhas near us on the floor,
so we can enjoy them next to us when we do our projects.

Kaitlyn was compelled to be near the Buddha figures displayed in my home.
She was careful in their presence and treated them as treasured friends.

Memories of My House

Kaitlyn had been coming to my house since she was born while her parents worked and, additionally, for regular weekend visits. I wanted her to always feel welcome and to know my house was her home too. She had her own bedroom, toys, and clothes. My two living room areas had her books, art supplies, blocks, and craft materials. I always provided activities for us to do, so our time together would be joyful and filled with child-friendly fun and educational events. The backyard was set up for her enjoyment, growth, and fun. She had a climber, tricycle, water table, and many toys to excite her imagination. And she had me, her grandma.

She and I were constant companions to each other. We had our herb garden to tend, taste, and create recipes or teas in the afternoon when we rested after lunch. We had our vegetable garden that Kaitlyn planted, watered, and watched grow. Kaitlyn selected the different varieties of tomatoes, eggplants, squash, and kale and planted them carefully in the garden. She loved caring for the plants and eating the gardens gifts.

When it was too cold outside for our comfort, we played together on the floor in the house. Sometimes, friends joined us and participated in our playtime fun. From the time Kaitlyn could sit on her own, she would point to the Buddha statues and insist that I put them on the floor. She was careful and gentle when she touched or got close to each Buddha. Kaitlyn found comfort in their presence. Our play circle was an atmosphere of calmness, thoughtfulness, and love for everyone and everything around us. Kaitlyn enjoyed this setting and thrived in it. She was happy and considerate of everyone and everything in our circle.

Kaitlyn Gem

Grandma, you need to be mindful when you walk outside.
Be careful not to step on bugs, gum, or garbage. Stop to
see all the lovely flowers. And don't fall down. You can get
hurt. We have only one body, and you must take care of it.

Kaitlyn shared her wisdom with me every day we were together, and we
were together almost every day. She valued life and simple adventures.
When she was little, we went for walks in the park in her stroller and
collected leaves, pine cones, and rocks. We reviewed and discussed our
treasures back at my house as we snuggled together on the couch. As she got
older, she effortlessly walked with me to the park, enjoying the hills, houses,
and wonders of the neighborhood. Kaitlyn and the outdoors were partners.

The Turning Point

I was ready to bring Kaitlyn home to my house after she achieved a sense of wellness following the home rehabilitation period. It was August, and the weather invited us to return to our neighborhood park. It contained so many joyous memories and opportunities for Kaitlyn's growth.

Before Kaitlyn was sick, she played on the playground equipment with the skills and grace of an agile child. She was fearless, and I worked with her on not being reckless. I regarded returning to the park as an achievement while living with brain cancer. We slowly and carefully walked the half-block climb, holding hands as usual. Kaitlyn commented on the familiar houses, the current flower displays, and the seasonal decorations she stored in her memory.

"Grandma, this house had the scariest decorations last year. Soon it will be Halloween, and they will put some crazy stuff out here again. Remember when this house had giant spiders and bloody hands coming up from the ground? I wasn't afraid."

When we got to the playground area, Kaitlyn attempted to play on the slide, swing, and balance beam and became quickly frustrated when her current body didn't afford her the skills to navigate and enjoy these once easily accessible activities. She shouted, "Grandma, I can't climb the ladder up the slide. It's difficult, and I'm tired."

I witnessed the progress and progression of her motor skills that she worked so diligently to achieve in the last four weeks. I totally misjudged her current abilities, as my frame of reference was muddled with hope and confidence that her new normal showed promise for a brighter future. I realized that Kaitlyn could never regain the competency she once enjoyed.

She remembered her body and the expertise she once claimed at her playground and longed for her strength and health as she cried, "I wish I never got a bump in my head. I hate my body."

I sat on the ground and wrapped my arms around her as she sat in my lap. I told her I wished the same thing, but I still loved her and her body. I thought about all we achieved since the radiation treatments, and it distracted my perception of her present abilities. She still carried twenty extra pounds. Her endurance and strength were severely compromised. And I had no way of fully comprehending her pain, visual acuity, and perceptual skills.

I told her, "I remember when I was little and playground equipment was difficult for me too."

She made a face that showed she was not comforted by my comment. I told her there were still many things to enjoy in the park. That didn't comfort her either.

I felt overwhelmed with sadness and wanted to cry at the realization of the tremendous loss we were both experiencing. I proceeded to tell my dear grandchild a story. "Kaitlyn, when you were just three years old and we were together playing at the park, you got this silly idea to run away from me. I screamed, 'Kaitlyn, stop! Kaitlyn, stop, as loud as I could. But you kept running. I ran after you super fast, not like an old grandma, but like a cat running after the kitten that got away and needed protection from her ridiculous self. I don't know if you pretended not to hear me or just followed your inner voice that told you to run free. And then, guess what? You stopped running."

Kaitlyn thoughtfully considered my story. She looked into my eyes and said, "Grandma, I will never run away from you again."

I knew at that moment I couldn't stop her from leaving, and we were ready to recognize the realness of her diagnosis. We sat huddled together under a tree quiet in our thoughts. As I held her in my arms, I felt a shift in both our perceptions of our new world. I sensed Kaitlyn accepted her life and impending death. I perceived she understood her future was going to be short-lived. It was heartbreaking to behold a five-year-old child concede that she couldn't win the fight for her life. It was surprisingly peaceful to contemplate her recognition that the DIPG diagnosis was a given on her life journey. The miracle I hoped for didn't happen the way I prayed for it, but we experienced a miracle that day.

Kaitlyn and I slowly and mindfully walked back to my house. That was our last visit to the park. We both learned that love and acceptance were necessary companions on this journey. And things were going to be different. She adapted to her needs and the care she now required for daily existence. She accepted her body and the conditions of her fate. She did not fight or resist the help she required from Elizabeth and me. She graciously accepted our assistance with tenderness and humor. She freely and frequently voiced her love and appreciation to us. We returned it with abundance.

Kaitlyn kept her promise and never ran away from me again. In three short months, she flew from me.

Kaitlyn Gem

Grandma, your house is my house too. I love being here. Everything I need is here. It's a perfect place for a kid and a grandma.

We can snuggle and rest when I get tired, play when I have energy, and visit neighbors when we need some extra love in our day. Everyone missed me when I was too sick to be here. And our friends know where you live, so they can visit us any time they want.

I was very happy Kaitlyn achieved a state of wellness to return with me to my home. I had a million memories of her in my house, and I wanted to make a million more.

Back at Grandma's House

Kaitlyn and her health needs were our first consideration as we approached each day. Then, we thoughtfully considered activities, day trips, and friend visits that we hoped would be enjoyable and fun. Elizabeth and I always included Kaitlyn in devising a day that she could look forward to and take joy in.

Kaitlyn frequently woke up feeling sick with head pain, nausea, and vomiting. Elizabeth and I did what was necessary to help her be comfortable. Usually a slow-paced morning with a light breakfast and her medications helped her transition from nighttime sleep to morning wake up. We adjusted her evening routine as well. When she appeared fatigued toward the end of the day, we offered an afternoon bath, an early dinner, and a bedtime to accommodate her weakened body and sleepy mind. There were nights Kaitlyn and I snuggled in bed ready to sleep when the sun was still shining, but her eyes needed to close.

I brought Kaitlyn to my house when she felt well enough. I kept a wheelchair there for the days when her legs were too weak to carry her. I kept her medicines in my bag to keep her as comfortable as possible.

My neighbor and friend Pam arrived at the door with amusing goodies she selected specifically for Kaitlyn's tastes and interests. Chocolate pudding was a huge hit for the child who loved eating. A cookie haunted house to decorate fit perfectly in our Halloween celebrations. The candy turkey cake provided hours of fun entertainment for Kaitlyn as she carefully selected each colorful sweet confection and placed it on the cake or in her mouth.

Back in April, when Kaitlyn was diagnosed with DIPG, Pam went to each home on the block to thoughtfully share the sad news about the joyful child who most people viewed over the years with me as my regular partner. My neighbors offered their love, prayers, and support during this sorrowful journey.

Pam kept Kaitlyn's vegetable garden growing and sent us pictures of its progress when we couldn't get there to see it. Pam and Kaitlyn shared an understanding of the significance of the garden. They both knew it represented the continuation of life even when facing illness and death. Pam committed herself to performing the necessary tasks to maintain stability in my home, such as caring for my dog when I was away and keeping my refrigerator well stocked with the ingredients I needed to make the soups Kaitlyn loved to eat.

Pam's husband, Ed, shared many encounters with Kaitlyn at the side wall of our backyards. Kaitlyn frequently stood at the wall to have a special exchange of vital information with Ed about nature. They both bonded in their love of flowers, trees, birds, and each other. They shared a devotion to the beauty found in the outdoors. I recall a memorable occasion when Ed fascinated Kaitlyn with a whistle sound he created blowing into a wisteria leaf. Kaitlyn enjoyed this simple pleasure and brought Ed a carefully selected leaf for him to produce this sound that intrigued her inventiveness. They both marveled at the unusual buzz and laughed as Kaitlyn attempted to produce it. She blew spit on the leaf, producing a soggy covering of saliva all over it and not a funny sound to be heard. Then she handed her leaf to Ed and said, "Here, you do it."

Ed laughed as he took her leaf and swiftly exchanged it for a dry one to entertain her with the comical noise.

My neighbors Jim and Barbara always delighted in visits with Kaitlyn, and she anticipated welcoming chats as we approached the home of these lovely people. Beautiful flowers surrounded their house, and Kaitlyn always stopped to admire the colorful display of the roses.

Kaitlyn felt comfortable exploring the front yard and announced to Barbara, "Jim is my boyfriend, and he always lets me run on the grass."

Kaitlyn united my neighborhood family with her innocence and love of the simple pleasures she discovered. She demonstrated that world beauty was always present. Kaitlyn effortlessly guided people to value their own childlike behaviors that would grant them happiness in life.

Kaitlyn and I devoted Tuesday afternoons to visiting our local growers' market. Our routine started with her placing five single dollar bills in her purse. Then she got a bag to put her vegetables in. After a short drive, we arrived at the outdoor marketplace ready to have an adventure. Kaitlyn would study each booth as if fine treasures were on display at the tables. The sellers delighted in Kaitlyn's comments and curiosity about their produce. They offered her samples to taste and gifts to put in her shopping bag that she carried over her shoulder with pride. She selected her vegetables with careful thought and took her possessions back home.

After she washed the goods outside at her water table, she brought them into the kitchen to contemplate her next move for this operation. Kaitlyn loved a recipe to roast vegetables and knew it effortlessly. She found the pan, olive oil, and cooking brush and demonstrated her competence and independence when cooking. I remained at her side if the task required Grandma's helping hand. Kaitlyn nibbled her foods as she prepared them and encouraged me to enjoy the taste too. I remember her bringing home a lemon cucumber, purple tomato, and patty pan squash with joy and excitement. Kaitlyn happily declared, "Grandma, I love the beautiful flavors."

As Kaitlyn's illness progressed and outside adventures became too tiring for her, we created happy home experiences. Friends visited and played with Kaitlyn for as long as she could endure. One day my friend Ardell entered into the house with a giant box of perfectly sized blocks. We sat on the floor building trains and creating objects that were inspired by our imaginations and involved us in an activity away from the world of cancer. We knew our time with Kaitlyn was limited, so we laughed loudly, played intensely, and treasured each moment as if it were going to be our last.

Kaitlyn Gem

Grandma, please take the necklaces I made for the doctors
so I can give them to the them. I need the doctors to help
me feel better. I think my gifts will make them happy and
help them feel better too.

Kaitlyn wanted to heal and live. She struggled with painful treatments yet
tolerated them because she hoped they would heal her. She demonstrated
her gratitude to the medical people involved in her care by making them
gifts that a five-year-old child treasures. She worked hard on creating
pictures, bracelets, and necklaces because she believed they carried the
power to put love into everyone's heart.

The Final Hospital Visit

We brought Kaitlyn to the hospital for the final time the beginning of November.

Elizabeth was contacted by the oncology clinic to take Kaitlyn for another brain scan in order to assess the progression of the cancerous tumor. She was advised that this was the standard protocol to follow and monitor her illness.

We had lived with Kaitlyn's illness since April and adjusted to her care while enjoying her personality and our flexible routines. Our love for Kaitlyn grew profoundly during this time, as we needed to put a lifetime of emotion into a brief seven-month space. And we had to store Kaitlyn's love into our being so it would nurture us throughout the rest of our life spans. There were days we almost forgot about the illness Kaitlyn carried, as we accepted the situation and flowed with our familiar routine.

Elizabeth, Kaitlyn, and I really didn't need a brain scan procedure to confirm what we already knew. Kaitlyn was struggling with her ability to walk, swallow, and stay focused. She required more medicines for pain management and nausea control. The brief three-month reprieve from severe symptoms was ending.

We assembled our appointment team of Grandpa, Elizabeth, Kaitlyn, and me and went to the hospital. Kaitlyn fiercely protested going there and made herself heard the entire car ride. She cried and complained that she was hungry and angry. She screamed that it interfered with her lunch, visit from friends, and playtime.

Kaitlyn wept. "Please let me stay home and watch the movie *Moana*. I don't need another hospital test."

It broke our hearts to force her to comply, especially when we already knew the dreaded results. I pushed Kaitlyn in her wheelchair, and she yelled at everyone who attempted to persuade her to cooperate. Her message was clear that she was not having this procedure. Elizabeth and I took turns entering the machine with Kaitlyn, hoping that if we could calm her, we could get the procedure completed. Kaitlyn absolutely refused to cooperate and made it impossible to get a still picture of her head.

After several attempts in and out of the machine, Elizabeth lifted Kaitlyn off the table and carried her away. Another medical test wasn't necessary to confirm what was evident. The machine wasn't smarter than the mother's observations and intuition. Kaitlyn was transitioning to the end of her life, and a medical test was not necessary to prove it. Elizabeth honored the shouts of her child and set Kaitlyn free from the medical procedure.

Apparently, there were enough pictures obtained during the scans for the oncologist to confirm what we all knew. The cancer had spread, and there was nothing more to do. Kaitlyn was dismissed from any more hospital tests or medical visits.

We left the hospital building exhausted. We already knew our precious girl was nearing the end of her life. We had no way of knowing exactly when that would be. We would continue to support and love our precious girl as long as she breathed.

As we walked away from the building, we felt a strange feeling of relief that the hospital visits and doctor appointments were over. We went home, and I cooked breakfast for dinner. Kaitlyn enjoyed this funny mix-up. We celebrated being together and enjoyed a simple meal.

Kaitlyn Gem

Grandma, I wonder who will come see me today. I hope
I don't have to get blood taken out of me. I'm a child, and
I need all my blood.

I love visitors. I show them my books and toys. I tell them
funny stories to make them laugh. But my body hurts so
much, and I don't want it to hurt anymore.

Elizabeth and I had to witness the pain and suffering Kaitlyn endured. She
was accurate in her words and perceptions. She gave some noble protests,
but mostly, she gave in to the inevitable misery dispensed on her little body
and her young mind.

Palliative/Hospice Care

Kaitlyn was eligible to get palliative care from the onset of her diagnosis and throughout the course of her treatment because DIPG is a terminal illness. Then the hospice care would be ready to assist her end-of-life needs. Elizabeth inquired about the service and was told a nurse would be assigned to Kaitlyn's care and visit our house at least once a week to monitor health, record vital signs, and answer questions. The nurse would consult with the doctor if more medical interventions were necessary.

Elizabeth requested palliative/hospice care in June when Kaitlyn experienced grievous symptoms and we needed medical support and guidance at home. We hoped the palliative/hospice care service would reduce laborious trips to the hospital. The home health assistance was a welcome relief as they managed medications and offered suggestions, while we remained in our familiar setting.

We anticipated that hospice care would be involved in the near future, and developing a positive relationship was imperative because we were going to share the most profound experience together. We wanted to allow Kaitlyn the opportunity to form a relationship with the special person who would be present to assist her with a peaceful and painless life transition.

The nurses quickly developed a relationship with Kaitlyn. They couldn't resist her charm and clever insights. We met all four nurses on the team, and one visited us weekly. Knowing the team gave us a security that a familiar face would always be available. Kaitlyn learned the unique personalities and styles of each nurse. She showed them her toys, told them stories, and accepted their treats as special gifts from new friends. Kaitlyn protested medical tests when needles were involved, but at least we were at home, and that seemed to provide comfort for her.

We recognized the difficult jobs these women signed up for and appreciated their service. The nurse who took care of Kaitlyn for the final days of her life was a compassionate soul who used love and tenderness to aid Kaitlyn on her journey from life to death. Her honesty and humanity will always be remembered.

Kaitlyn Gem

Grandma, the cemetery is a beautiful place. It is peaceful,
and everyone who comes here brings flowers and thinks
about the person they came to see. They still love them,
and you will always love me too.

Kaitlyn was not afraid to die. She understood that it was the natural
process of all living beings. A few days before Kaitlyn passed, she told her
mom and me several times that her body was too sick to live in anymore.
She was dizzy, felt nauseated, was in pain, had difficulty swallowing, and
couldn't walk. Thankfully, she could still talk. We could enjoy her words
of wisdom, her hugs and kisses, and her sweet breath.

Kaitlyn Knew

Kaitlyn declared to me about a month before she was diagnosed with DIPG her knowing and her burial wishes. We were riding in my car, and she asked in her little girl voice, "Grandma, what happens to the body after a person dies?"

I explained to Kaitlyn some various methods I knew about, such as cremation, burial in a coffin, or donation of the body to science. Kaitlyn continued the conversation and asked, "Grandma, can you please show me a cemetery?"

I viewed this conversation as an educational opportunity for a curious child. I drove to a nearby cemetery, and we walked along the paved path that led to the burial area. Kaitlyn looked around and commented on the lovely flowers and very green grass. She noticed the words inscribed on the headstones and asked me to read several out loud. Then she announced, "When I die, I want to be cremated, have my ashes placed in a box, bury it in the ground, and bring me pink and yellow flowers when you come to visit."

I explained to Kaitlyn that I was much older than she, so I would die first, and she could visit me with the pretty flowers. Kaitlyn did not reply. She obviously had a secret that I was not ready to hear. But on that day, her knowledge about her fate was revealed.

I expressed this experience to Elizabeth after Kaitlyn received the cancer diagnosis and she was tranquilly asleep in her hospital bed. I knew

Elizabeth would honor her child's wishes when the time came to make these arrangements. There was a calm in knowing Kaitlyn participated in this choice.

Kaitlyn perceived the plan already set. She sensed on a sunny day in March, about a month before we even heard about DIPG, what was soon to be revealed. Kaitlyn understood and accepted her life journey. I hoped I could follow her lead.

Kaitlyn Gem

Grandma, if all the children in the world were lined up for
you to choose a granddaughter, you would always pick me.
If all the mommies in the world were lined up, I would pick
my mommy. And Mommy picked you to be my grandma.
We are a forever team.

Kaitlyn knew she was loved. Our team was everlasting. She was absolutely
correct. This beautiful little person taught us about love and life. Her
lessons enriched our soul's purpose. Kaitlyn was a blessing.

Final Weeks

Kaitlyn's illness seemed to rapidly progress. Her movements were slower, her appetite sharply decreased, and her waking hours were filled with outbursts of misery. We strived to create enjoyable moments with family and friends as we assembled for short visits. We carefully monitored her needs and attempted to anticipate when more pain medicines were necessary to help avoid explosive tantrums.

I slept with Kaitlyn every night, so she was never alone. I cared for her needs that crept into the darkness as sleep became difficult and body functions, pain, and fears visited us. I held her in my arms and answered her questions, told her stories, and listened to her thoughts and ideas about life and death. She reassured me that she was a brave child who didn't want to die but knew her body was too sick to live. She expressed that her life was great and filled with love and adventures.

She also told me I should be brave and not let fear stop me from exciting experiences. She recalled a time I had forbidden her to run down a steep hill. She wanted me to know she was not afraid to perform the challenge of the hill, and she was rather capable of mastering this triumph.

I was grateful she shared this with me because it gave me an opportunity to have a creative redo. I told her to hold my hand and close her eyes and imagine we were now racing down the hill together. I counted to three and said, "Let's go." When I asked her if she enjoyed our fantastic visionary adventure, she smiled and kissed my face.

Kaitlyn and I loved to listen to guided meditations that I played on my cell phone. This was an activity we had done every morning as we started our day since she was three years old. The meditations gave us a chance to enter each new day in a gracious and serene aura. We added the beautiful and calming meditations to our bedtime routine, and it was natural for us to drift into sleep holding each other as we listened to the soothing music, gentle voices, and kind words.

I was grateful each morning when we awoke and welcomed another day to live with Kaitlyn in the physical world. Kaitlyn, Mommy, Gray the cat, and I greeted visitors who joined us and filled the final days of Kaitlyn's life with love and unity. We were all cognizant these moments were precious gifts and blessings we needed to treasure.

Elizabeth and I reserved sobbing for private moments when we needed to release our sadness in the easy flow of tears. We faithfully savored and embraced every living second with Kaitlyn. We quietly understood that time was no longer our friend, and the experiences we valued beyond measure would soon terminate. We would have to physically part with the greatest love we had ever known. We recognized that extreme sadness would hold a place in our future. We appreciated that we must survive so Kaitlyn could live as we carried her love in our hearts. We believed that through us, and all the people who entered this journey with us, Kaitlyn would continue to touch people and continue to make a difference in the world.

Kaitlyn told me when she was four years old, before brain cancer entered our world, that when she grew up, she wanted to be a heart surgeon. My granddaughter ingeniously achieved her goal. She opened so many hearts and filled them with love. Kaitlyn did a tremendous job in her short and purposeful life. Each individual touched by her love has the imperative responsibility to honor the heavenly gift that Kaitlyn intentionally presented to them.

Kaitlyn Gem

> Grandma, I really don't like hospitals. Please promise me
> no more hospitals.

That promise was made and kept. Kaitlyn died at home, in her bed, with her mother, grandfather, and me holding her and loving her before she took her final breath and parted from her body.

The Final Days

Kaitlyn lost almost all her body functions overnight. When she woke up on Monday, November 20, 2017, she could not swallow or willfully move her body. The oral medications were useless and dripped out of her mouth. She couldn't even sit in her bed with support. Her speech was reduced to single word utterances that she labored to emit. As she lay on her pillow, her face grimaced and revealed the horrific pain and torment from her state of being.

Elizabeth reported what she observed to the hospice nurse. She requested medications that could be administered through the port in Kaitlyn's chest so her child could have some relief. When the nurse arrived, she watched and noted what we already knew. She heard Kaitlyn's labored breath and witnessed her inability to speak. She saw the extreme pain Kaitlyn was experiencing. It was agreed that the time to access the port had come. Kaitlyn deserved to be freed from the stabbing pain in her head. Kaitlyn's end of life was now upon us.

Elizabeth held her child as the nurse inserted the needle into the port in Kaitlyn's chest. She quickly responded to the continuous flow of medication and looked as if she were resting in her bed in a tranquil state of calm and peace. We glimpsed little smiles, a relaxed face, and her beautiful blue eyes that opened to acknowledge her awareness of our presence and closed for her to rest. Elizabeth, Gray the cat, and I stayed in the bed with Kaitlyn, recalling fun memories of her childhood and expressing our eternal love to her. She listened and watched us with her penetrating eyes and open heart.

Kaitlyn's beloved grandfather, the man she called Papa, sat with her and told her stories about love, life, and beyond. She was soothed by his voice, and he was grateful to have a few more moments to treasure with his precious granddaughter.

The hospice nurse notified us when she believed death was coming for Kaitlyn. We sat with her on the bed quietly weeping and not daring to blink as we watched her breathe in a strange manner. It was loud, rapid, and even. It was difficult to know if her breath was an attempt to live another moment or an effort to free herself from her body. We witnessed her lift her paralyzed right arm to touch her mommy's face before she took her final breath. We were with her as she completed this life's journey.

Life with Great Sadness and Abundant Love

Elizabeth and I, in a state of bewilderment, gathered with Papa and Uncle Jason to share stories and memories of Kaitlyn's short life as we buried her ashes in a small box. We put our fingerprints on the little box that carried her remains as it was carefully placed into the ground in a cemetery close to our home. We put yellow and pink flowers on the ground above her. We felt her presence around us from the moment she passed, and on many occasions, we believed she was just a flicker away.

Kaitlyn died in the manner everyone hopes to have at the end of his or her life. She was surrounded by the people who loved her. She looked peaceful and beautiful. If she was one hundred years old, we would have said her life was completed and filled with meaning and joy. She was only five years old, and that's the struggle.

Kaitlyn did have a life filled with meaning and joy. But it was a short life and incompatible with expectations. Her actual passing was calm. There was a strange sense of relief that her struggle with illness was over. She was free of pain and released from the body that did not serve her spirit any longer. We knew the end of the story on the day she was diagnosed with DIPG seven months earlier, and like every story, it came to an end. We must now live our life journey without Kaitlyn.

We had a celebration of Kaitlyn's life with family and friends a few days after the burial. We gathered for an occasion of shared grief and love for the little girl who swiftly learned the meaning of life and proceeded on her next passage.

I moved back to my house, and Elizabeth moved into a townhouse with Gray, the kitty. Elizabeth sold the house that she and Kaitlyn shared. A dear friend, Donna, gave her real estate expertise and guidance to make the sale painless and quick.

Elizabeth and I are faithfully committed to each other and keep Kaitlyn's stories ever present as we recall details of the child we bonded with and loved and never thought would have departed so soon. Our love for each other and Kaitlyn remains strong. The grief grips us like an invisible body part attached to our being and may remain forever. It is my hope that time will lessen the pain of this additional appendage and positive experiences will be welcomed next to our grief.

On the gravestone, Elizabeth had the words inscribed, "We Love You To Infinity." We frequently heard Kaitlyn say this to us, and it seemed fitting to eternalize it on the headstone that marks the place where her ashes rest.

Elizabeth had necklaces made for us of the infinity symbol. The jeweler, Joe at Mark Diamond, listened to the Kaitlyn story as Elizabeth told it with honor and heartbreak.

Elizabeth explained, "I have these diamonds that I was saving to give my daughter. She died four months ago. I am hoping you could put them into necklaces with the infinity symbol. Yes, we want two infinities. One necklace for my mom and one for me."

He joined our journey and created artful matching necklaces for us with Kaitlyn's name and birthstone on the back of the necklace, worn against our skin, and diamonds on the front to signify our everlasting love.

I planted the edible garden in the spring to continue the tradition Kaitlyn valued. I felt her beautiful presence as she approved my selection of herbs and vegetables. I shared the Kaitlyn story with the owner of a landscape business, Brent, who appeared inspired by the narrative and assisted me in preparing the soil to help create the foundation of a bountiful garden. When his work was completed, we sat down together and looked at pictures of Kaitlyn. I felt the Kaitlyn energy with us as the gentle man looked and listened. I appreciated his time, work, and kindness.

I joined a weekly support circle to share my Kaitlyn story with a sympathetic group of people who understood the agony of grief. We nurture our bereaved souls as we gather together to achieve acceptance and adjustment to the world missing our special someone. Our bond unites us in a community free from judgement in an atmosphere safe to share our hearts. We assemble together in a demonstration of allegiance and shared humanity. We share hugs, kisses, tears, and laughter as we tell our stories. We all know that loss is part of the human experience. We understand that love and tenderness are our only choices in relating to each other. We respect that everyone's journey in grief is different and the same.

I wonder if I will always wake each morning and feel the agony and depletion of the passing of my precious granddaughter. When Kaitlyn was alive, I faced each day with anticipation and vigor that coincided with being next to the child I loved. Kaitlyn taught me life lessons, and I promised her I would be a good listener and share her truths. I affirmed I would continue on my life journey with her ever present in my soul. I vowed that I would carry her love in my heart. I professed I would never forget the beautiful child who graced me for five and a half years with her love, wisdom, and childish antics and then left her body for her next journey. She bestowed upon me an enduring love to carry and treasure forever. I realize time is not a valid measure of a life.

Yes, her life was completed and filled with meaning and joy.

Part Two

Grandma Gem

Kaitlyn, I am writing a book to tell the world about you. I was blessed to love and cherish you for the five years you lived. Now, my love for you continues and grows in my thoughts, dreams, and prayers. I will forever remember the connection you and I created. We wove a magnificent bond that affirmed our unique talents and personalities. I am slowly adjusting to our new and different relationship. Our love remains intact, strong, and infinite.

The Book Two Infinities

This book has served as a platform to remember and record highlights of my granddaughter. Her short life story impacted my world beyond measure. Examining the recent past with Kaitlyn indulged me to relive and capture detailed moments and feelings so I could give testimony to her existence. My mind revived her laughter, struggles, and tears and created private, living images of her. I mentally controlled her exit and keep her just a thought away.

I will always have a book to treasure when the memories fade because I'm certain time will do that. I will never release my love for Kaitlyn from my heart. Time becomes the enemy and the protector. As each day dawns, I move away from grief, and the pain lessens. My fear is the memories will lesson too. I hope the book will free me from griping tightly to the memorization of details and serve as a corroborator with my mind. Nothing and no one could ever replace Kaitlyn. A book devoted to her story ignites my imagination and honors the person I loved so deeply and completely.

Kaitlyn's death interrupted plans and goals, forcing an abrupt adjustment to the world without her physical presence. I was Grandma, the unconditional love source for this child. She was my collaborator in everyday events. I am forced now on a path to navigate without my constant companion and find a new trail with purpose and meaning.

My grief can be described as a thorn that periodically stabs me. It lingers like an unwelcome intruder I cannot seem to release. I graciously accept periods of peace that embrace me and trust these episodes will expand. I grow in the direction of acceptance, remembering the gifts Kaitlyn granted to me were boundless and sustainable for a lifetime. I gratefully acknowledge that five years of love with her was a legacy to treasure forever. My mind, body, and spirit are operative in a process to obtain alignment and balance. I am committed to integrating the lessons taught to me from my granddaughter.

I intend for this book to serve as a celebration of Kaitlyn's life—a confirmation of her existence, individuality, and unique gifts and a remembrance for the deep love I got to experience with this child. I ache for her physical body and deeply miss the hugs and kisses she dispensed on me. I recall her sweet inflections, intonations, and expressions and pray I will always have the flashbacks of her voice in my head. I laugh at the funny mischief of a five-year-old child who proved that wisdom and humor were excellent teachers.

I read selected passages from my book to people who visit my home. I entrust with them the Kaitlyn story as recorded from my memory. I articulate my heartfelt words and observe the reactions from the audience who also treasured her life and want to reminisce about her love and life. As I examine passages aloud to friends, or in silence to myself, I periodically stop, pause, and weep at a section that floods my soul with complex emotions. I observe that my book is important to many people who knew her. We laugh and cry together, letting our thoughts embrace recollections of the little girl who was sassy, smart, and beautiful but suffered and died too soon. I feel connected with the people who visit, and as I recapture valued memories, I know we are bonded in love.

I hope this book also serves people I don't know—the individuals who are connected to me because of similar experiences or common interests or who are simply drawn to read it; the folks who know about the heartbreak of cancer, the loss of a grandchild, the grief associated with the death of a loved one, or just relate because they are fellow humans.

This book is also a gift to give my daughter, Elizabeth. I have profound respect and high regard for her. She did not crumble from her broken heart but rather searched for wisdom, strength, and meaning in this complicated life episode. I witnessed her intense and endless love for her child during Kaitlyn's entire life and now beyond. She utilized her intelligence when dealing with medical personnel and health issues. She demonstrated confidence as she ministered to her child. Her constant love gave Kaitlyn a comfort and trust in the world that could be confusing and painful. My daughter's authentic mothering helped me feel grounded and find my place on this journey. Our cycle of love bonds our souls forever.

I never expected to endure this life transformation or to be forced to accept and navigate this passage and outcome. I believed that a child dying was unnatural and unimagined. This occurrence validates the preciousness and fragility of being alive. I never conceived that I would be forced to give testimony or witness Kaitlyn as the star participant in a grievous tale. A book will never replace her, but it can serve to recall and honor her.

Essentially, I desire to always remember and treasure the relationship I shared with the child I loved completely. As I celebrate her life and recollect her death, I hope to share her truth.

Grandma Gem

Kaitlyn, the vegetable garden is growing wild. You must be the garden fairy watching and protecting each blossom, leaf, stem, root, and fruit. I spied one perfectly formed and ripened cherry tomato. I gingerly picked it, brought it home, and ate it. Thank you for teaching me to rejoice in the fruits of the earth.

The Gardener and the Garden

My longtime friend Pat insisted, "Kaitlyn came to us to be our teacher. It is our job to learn and accept the gifts of her wisdom."

Pat was my person to rant and rave to about the injustices of the Kaitlyn situation. She provided the sympathetic ear when I needed to be heard and always reminded me that I had the strength to continue when I was overwhelmed with grief about the inevitable outcome. I was fortunate to have many friends in my corner offering their support and love.

My neighbor and friend Ed watched as I planted the garden. He offered assistance, kindness, and love as I shed many tears when I was surrounded by the soil, plants, and tools in the area filled with Kaitlyn memories.

Kaitlyn loved this task. She understood the care necessary to grow a beautiful garden and respected the journey. She got to experience planting and growing a garden for two seasons. She learned that growing plants presented a commitment that can be compared to any challenge that required trust in the unknown. It is an endeavor entered with hope and faith for a wonderful outcome. It requires a devotion of time, nourishment, and patience. It is like a magical undertaking, watching your labor take form and produce a splendor of gifts to ingest and feed upon. The life cycle is enacted in front of you, and each stage is a miracle of nature. The entire journey unfolds to witness, celebrate, guide, and put to rest.

I was so overjoyed when Kaitlyn arrived in our family. Her beautiful blue eyes revealed an amazing soul that knew about the depth of love. When she was a baby, she was comfortable in the world. She loved to eat, cuddle, look, and listen. She appreciated nature, people, and new experiences. She was a child who expressed her opinions and observations without hesitation in a confident manner.

It's no wonder my sadness is profound and deep from her death. My imagination never went to a time when I would live and Kaitlyn would not. I believed that the natural order of life proclaimed that children outlive their parents, and certainly their grandmother. Kaitlyn's death at five years old challenged my perception of the world.

When I truthfully reviewed how I cared for Kaitlyn, I was forced to admit that the knowledge of how frail life can be prevailed in my treatment of our daily existence. I followed rules to protect Kaitlyn from injury and harm. I wanted her to eat well, learn how to be safe, and know how to make decisions in a world that was filled with uncertain choices. I attempted to prevent accidents from occurring, treated sicknesses with educated care, and took precautions to provide an environment free from harm for the precious person entrusted in my care.

I wanted to teach her, as best as I could, to love herself and value her heart, body, and spirit. I now feel compelled to examine my approach, as I relinquish control of the life cycle.

When I shared this thought with my daughter, she wisely declared, "You needed to keep Kaitlyn as safe as humanly possible. That is the responsibility of parents, grandparents, and any caretaker of children."

I now realize my control was limited and perhaps an illusion. I am forced into an acceptance of Kaitlyn's shortened life—a new world that shattered my perception that children don't die before they live a long time. I did my best to protect and guide Kaitlyn. I did it with love and intelligence. I tried to present to her a life that was enriched with opportunity to grow, actualize, and enjoy love and learning. I wanted her to have meaningful relationships and true fun.

I alone am the gardener who tends to the soil, waits for the plants to grow, and celebrates the harvest accepting the outcome with its gifts. I must accept that one huge hailstorm can destroy all the precious growth. Kaitlyn's hailstorm was childhood cancer, a grievous event that swiped a young life and took the child I loved.

Elizabeth told me cancer did not kill Kaitlyn. Cancer freed Kaitlyn from her physical body to journey on. This reframing of the cancer narrative makes space for acceptance. It denounces the powerful cancer enemy. Elizabeth refuses to give cancer any more power. She will not be a second victim to this cancer invasion. Elizabeth longs for the physical Kaitlyn and the joy of having a daughter to love and watch develop through all the stages of life. She grieves for the person she birthed and believed would be there to watch and guide as she grew up. She is forced into expanding her perception of life, love, and faith. Her relationship with Kaitlyn will never die. Elizabeth will strive to live a meaningful, thoughtful, and spiritual life.

We live in a world where many families feel the impact of cancer. It can change a life in an instant. The pain and suffering of the cancer diagnosis presents a heartbreaking journey into medications, procedures, suffering, and even death. I was the witness of a cancer invasion. I look at my daughter, and once again, I am compelled by her wisdom to celebrate Kaitlyn as my gardener and my garden.

Grandma Gem

Kaitlyn, if all the children in the world were in a line and I could pick one to be my granddaughter, it would be you. Even if I had superpowers and knowledge of the future, I would not hesitate to have you be the little girl to call me Grandma. Mommy and I are certain that five years of life with you were a boundless gift that continues to present itself in everything we do. We comfort and guide each other to nourish the love we treasured with you. You were a beautiful child who loved her name and cherished her life. Thank you for your love.

A Trip to Honor Kaitlyn

Elizabeth and I went to Alaska eight months into our grief journey. We set out to see the beauty of nature that Kaitlyn valued so highly. The whales, eagles, and trees were there to love, appreciate, and value as living beings sharing the planet with us. We looked at the amazing sky that remained lit up until midnight when the sun completed setting. We celebrated Kaitlyn in everything we did and viewed.

We sat with different people when we had our breakfast and lunch, and my motherly pride overflowed when I heard Elizabeth speak to the men and women at our table. She gracefully shared, "My daughter died this past November. She was five years old. My mom and I are on this trip to honor her life and her love of nature. We are respecting the promise we made to her to go to Alaska and bring her with us. We wear our infinity necklaces as tokens that remind us of her clever conversations that expressed her deep understanding of love. Kaitlyn always told us she loved us to infinity and two infinities."

Grandma Gem

Kaitlyn, each morning when I wake up, I reach for my journal and record three things. First, I write my dream. I believe my nighttime visions reveal valuable information. I wake up happy when I had a visit from you during the night. Then I write the gratitude I feel that morning. Having you in my life to share a love connection is always first on my list. Then I write my seeds. They are the prayers for peace, love, and joy in the world. They are my hopes and dreams for the people I know and love. They hold the promise of a beautiful future. I look for you in all the beauty I witness. I want to make you proud of me as I carry your love in my heart exactly where you put it.

I love you to two infinities too!